Creative GIFTWRAPS

LARK BOOKS

A DIVISION OF STERLING PUBLISHING CO., INC.
NEW YORK

Creative GIFTWRAPS

IDEAS AND INSPIRATIONS, TIPS AND TECHNIQUES

Constance E. Richards

Art Director: Celia Naranjo

Production Assistant: Hannes Charen

Assistant Editor: Catharine Sutherland

Photographers: Evan Bracken, Richard Hasselberg

Illustrations: Vadim Bora

Library of Congress Cataloging-in-Publishing Data

Richards, Constance E.
      Creative giftwraps : ideas and inspirations, tips and techniques /
  Constance E. Richards.
        p. cm.
     ISBN 1-57990-154-9
     1. Gift wrapping. I. Title.
  TT870.R53 2000
  745.54—DC21   99-44190
                                      CIP

10 9 8 7 6 5 4 3 2 1

First Edition

Published by Lark Books,
a division of Sterling Publishing Co., Inc.
387 Park Avenue South, New York, N.Y. 10016

© 2000, Lark Books
Distributed in Canada by Sterling Publishing,
c/o Canadian Manda Group, One Atlantic Ave., Suite 105
Toronto, Ontario, Canada M6K 3E7

Distributed in Australia by Capricorn Link (Australia) Pty Ltd., P.O. Box 6651,
Baulkham Hills, Business Centre NSW 2153, Australia

If you have questions or comments about this book, please contact:
Lark Books
50 College St.
Asheville, NC 28801
(828) 253-0467

Printed in Hong Kong by H&Y Printing Ltd.

ISBN 1-57990-154-9

Acknowledgments

Many thanks to all of the incredibly talented designers and artists who contributed projects to this book. Professionals in their own field, they applied their knowledge and skills of their chosen medium to the art of gift wrapping.

A special thanks to Mary Worrell and Chuck Carmichael for the use of their wonderful home in Asheville, NC, which provided the perfect backdrop for many of our lavish gift wraps. The banana bread was great, too. Thank you also to Elizabeth McGillivray for the use of her apartment and balcony. A special *spasibo* to artist and sculptor Vadim Bora for the graceful sketches he created for this book, as well as for his willingness to create wrappings and decorations to order, and for his uncomplaining assistance in transporting delicately wrapped packages from set to set. To our wonderful "bow lady" Brinda Caldwell—a big thank you for consulting on our step-by-step bow-making and gift-wrapping basics. Thank you to Molly Sieburg and The Gardener's Cottage in Asheville, NC for stepping in and creating big hits with her gorgeous leaves and flowers, using her artistic flair. We thank Heiwa restaurant and The Natural Home, also in downtown Asheville, for the lending of props.

Last, but certainly not least, a thousand thanks each for art director Celia Naranjo for her beautiful photo arrangements and fantastic design of this book, and to Evan Bracken for his exceptional photography and patience. Additional thanks to Catharine Sutherland for her excellent research. A sincere thank you to Deborah Morgenthal for her assistance and advice on many aspects of this book.

Thanks go to the following for early inspiration: Ken Richards, who will probably still wrap presents in masking tape and brown paper bags; and to Irene Richards, for instilling the art of crisp corners, neat bows, and recycled wrapping paper.

Contents

OURS IS A GIFT-GIVING SOCIETY. We give gifts to loved ones, friends, relatives, bosses, and others to show appreciation, adoration, gratitude, respect, joy, or to celebrate a special occasion. Be the gift expensive or a

INTRODUCTION

small token, we generally enclose it in some fashion, temporarily hiding it from view until the receiver tears into the wrapping, revealing its contents with glee.

One may argue, why then bother at all with a wrapping, if it is simply a means to an end? Try thinking of giftwrap as a part of the gift within. This outer decorative sheath may hint at what's inside, or it may impart the

type of celebration that this gift is honoring. The wrapping may say something about the bearer of the gift or about the recipient. It certainly says something about the gift giver's taste.

Presentation, after all, is a gift's first message. You may spend hours agonizing over the perfect gift. Yet, if you merely plaster some sheets of wrinkled paper together with sticky tape and slap a rumpled bow on top of it all, you've changed the message completely.

What was once a
thoughtful present ap-
pears to be a hastily
pulled-together last-
minute purchase,
canceling out the care
you put into choosing the
gift in the first place.

 With just a few
basic creases and folds
or twists and loops, your wrapping can turn the mundane into the fabulous.
Garnishing plain paper with an embellishment or two using natural materials, can brighten a package in minutes. A finely folded bow conveys elegance
and grandeur. A miniature object or handmade card can hint at the gift inside. Of course, if wrapping seems too much of a bother to you, a gift

The best of all gifts is the good intention of the giver.   —Latin Proverb

container may be just the thing; how about a bag, box, or piece of fabric,
that is a complete wrapping unto itself? Boxes and bags can be used again
and again, and a fine-looking gift box can later be used to store photographs,
jewelry, recipes, bills, or knickknacks.

 The refined Asian art of gift giving and wrapping is especially entic-
ing; with its centuries-old tradition of delicate rice-paper or bamboo-leaf
wrappings, origami ornamentation, and folded fabric casings, gift wrapping

is elevated to an art form. If this sounds daunting, try using a square of fabric, a pretty scarf, or even a handkerchief to disguise your gift. You will read how, in the following pages.

Today there are scores of commercial papers on the market—many of them quite wonderful. So feel free to pick and choose from them to your heart's content. You can jazz up commercial wrapping by adding a spectacular bow or a colorful array of ribbons—perhaps tying miniature bows all over the gift.

Wrapping gifts should be a joy, not a chore. Inspiration begets inspiration, so get out those scissors and tape, a little glue, some fabric, some twigs, nuts, buttons, leaves....oh, we could go on!

Enjoy this creative process, and share the pleasure of the generous spirit of giving.

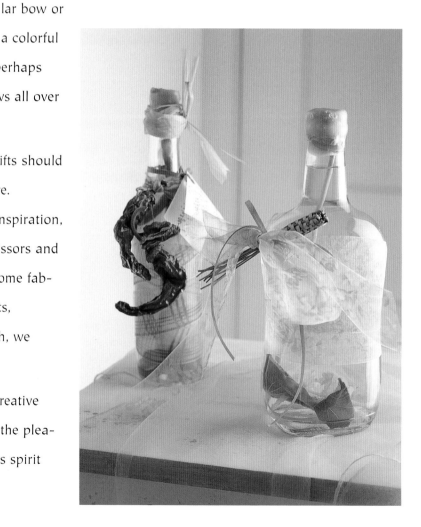

LEARN TO STRETCH YOUR IMAGINATION on the subject of gift wrapping. Think paper, cloth, the glossy pages of a magazine, a scarf, wallpaper, cardboard; look around your house and see what you might have lying around. You may find dried flowers, yarn, stamps, paint, buttons, and many other materials which you can incorporate in your giftwrap. All you need is some tape and scissors, and you are well on your way to creating fabulous giftwraps.

THE BASICS

PAPER

Commercial Wrapping Paper. So many excellent quality wrapping papers are available in stores these days. It's often hard to choose, but there's no reason you shouldn't buy commercial paper. You will have to be the judge of the type of paper you would like to use—be it an expensive designer paper, dollar store foil paper, and everything in between. Expensive doesn't always mean better, though. Think of the many variables: thinner paper will work better on smaller gifts; if your wrapped gift must be packed or travel with you, you'll need a thick and sturdy paper. While paper shopping, besides matching the paper to the occasion, try finding paper which conveys something personal to the gift receiver—perhaps a color he or she likes, a pattern which hints at what's wrapped inside, or a symbol which speaks to the receiver. Above all, don't be afraid to add personal touches to your store-bought paper. After all, that's what makes the difference between mediocre gift wrapping and fabulous giftwraps.

Tissue Paper. You most often find delicate tissue paper lining the interior of gift boxes or cushioning a present in a gift bag. Plain white

Your Materials

Develop a signature wrapping style. Try one color scheme using various designs.

paper has given way to wonderfully patterned tissue paper in numerous hues. Try wrapping small gifts in tissue. The paper will easily fold around small edges and corners. Be careful when transporting tissue-wrapped gifts, however; the paper is delicate and can wrinkle or tear.

Crepe Paper. Remember twisted crepe paper streamers at birthday parties of days gone by? Colorful crepe paper is still around, and large sheets of this pliable material easily conform to awkward shapes. Take note, however; crepe paper is exceptionally sensitive to moisture. Once you have wrapped a package with this porous paper, don't leave it lying around for long, especially if the weather is damp. The paper tends to absorb moisture from the air and will pucker.

Choose from a variety of commercial or handmade papers.

Brown Paper. Say "paper" on your next trip to the checkout at the grocery store. Simple brown paper bags work well for a number of natural wrapping styles. Large boxes, especially, fare well with this thick paper. Heavy enough to withstand various glued decorations, brown paper is a great canvas for your creativity.

Cellophane Paper. You can find clear cellophane at craft-supply stores, florists, and sometimes grocery stores. Increasingly, however, colorful cellophane can be unearthed in these same places. This crinkly, flexible, and slippery paper is best used for odd-shaped or round objects. Gather several layers of different colors of cellophane around the gift, enclosing it completely and tying it off with ribbon. Leave plenty of paper gathered beyond the tying-off point and arrange the "plumes" artfully on top. The paper is usually stiff enough to hold itself up.

Handmade paper. Most handmade paper, the kind most often used in bookmaking and other crafts, is available at art-supply stores or through mail-order catalogs. There are so many varieties of handmade paper—colors, textures, density, design, and more—that you could easily buy out the whole store. Handmade paper will be more expensive than any of the other papers you buy; however, the effect is probably worth it. Try buying a few sheets of your favorite handmade paper, but use it to decorate your plain paper, rather than wrap the entire gift with it. Wrap a narrow piece around the center of a plainly wrapped package or wrap just a corner. Create a glorious accent, without breaking the bank. If you would really like to make an impression, or if your gift is expensive jewelry or a collector's item, then the wrapping deserves to be just as fine.

Decorating Your Own Paper. One of the most exciting types of gift wrap is the kind you make yourself. Sometimes you might end up making your own wrapping paper, simply because you've run out of time (see our Emergency Wrapping). But hopefully, you will enjoy this creative process and be able to develop your own style as you go. Try painting designs on paper with acrylic paints; use dimensional paints to hand draw patterns; the old standby of potato-stamping still works, too! Commercial stamps are so popular now that you'll have little problem finding the perfect one for your designs.

Homemade paper and gift tags are not only fun to receive, but fun to make. Use old-fashioned potato stamps or commercial stamps for a variety of designs on your gift paper and packages.

GIFT BAGS

So convenient, gift bags have become the end-all for many people. Just grab a pre-decorated bag in any size, toss in some tissue paper, and you're done. This is a relatively good idea—commercial bags can be very attractive, but you won't always have time to run out to the store before a special occasion, and few people keep a stash of bags on hand. For starters, they're fairly expensive, and unless you keep them hanging up, they can easily become crumpled or creased. And finally, unless your gift has been wrapped and then placed in the bag, you've robbed your friends of the joy of tearing into a covered package. That said, you can't deny the convenience of gift bags, so here's an idea. Rather than pay a fortune for commercially decorated bags, use those little bags with handles in which you've carried home a purchase. Cut a design out of decorative paper and glue it over the shops' name or brand name on the bag. You may wish to add a tied bundle of incense, dried grasses or flowers, or a raffia bow to the front, using a dab of tacky glue to secure the bundle.

Personalize gift bags by drawing designs on them with dimensional paints.

Often, party stores will run a sale on plain paper bags in a variety of colors, to get ready for the next season's designs and colors. Grab an armful of these, and decorate them yourself. A metallic marker works well—try writing your congratulations on the outside of the bag. Dimensional paints, found in craft-supply stores, can add an element of texture and color. Draw a series of symmetrical designs on either side of the bag. You may use a template, or go at it freehand.

Rubber stamps are also a great way to decorate plain bags. Are you a collector of decorative stamps? Coordinate the color of your ink with the bag, and stamp your favorite designs on top. The same can be done with plain boxes and envelopes.

EMERGENCY WRAPPING

So you're stuck at home or at the office and must come up with gift wrap immediately. No time even to pick up a gift bag at a drug store. What to do? In the office, let the copier be your friend. If you are presenting gifts to a close friend, enlarge and copy a photo of yourself and use this as your wrapping paper. Or arrange paper clips, scissors, a ruler, and any number of typical office supplies onto the copier plate, place a sheet of plain paper over that, and make a copy, preferably onto the largest paper available. Wrap your gift, with the images of the arranged clerical paraphernalia on top. Link together a string of paper clips and wrap it around the gift, linking the last clip on the strand with the first, so that it lies flush against the gift wrap. Patterns or pictures from your computer color printer also work well.

The easiest and most attractive wrap in an emergency, by far, are the glossy pages of a magazine. The paper is crisp and unwrinkled and creates a smooth and sleek wrapping. You may want to forgo any type of bow altogether, letting the images and plain lines speak for themselves.

The glossy pages of a magazine create this spectacular wrapping. Great for emergencies, or just for an interesting change from commercial paper, fashion or travel magazines supply the best variety of colors and scenes.

Paper napkins make another wonderful emergency wrap. Do you use brightly designed dinner or cocktail napkins? If your gift is fairly small in size, grab a napkin and wrap your gift with the colorful side out. If you don't have tape, the folds can be adhered together with one swipe of a glue stick.

The more you look around your house, the more you will be able to find great possibilities for emergency gift wrap. We give you several innovative examples, but don't be shy—stretch your imagination. You may even come up with enough ideas for a book of your own!

Look in your pantry for more emergency wraps. Colorful paper dinner napkins and even paper towels will work in a pinch. Affix kitchen trinkets in place of bows.

RIBBON

Lace. Bolts of lace from a sewing shop work just as well as lace ribbon bought in a gift store. The delicate material is best used in trimming a gift box, rather than for making bows, since the loosely woven lace won't hold its shape well.

Paper Ribbon. Paper ribbons are the most common and inexpensive ribbon found in stores. They run the spectrum from curly ribbon to textured twisted paper, which can be unwound into a wider crinkled ribbon.

Raffia. Raffia is a type of paper ribbon as well, often sold in its natural straw color. It's wonderful for wrapping bundles of flowers which you

The rich texture of twisted or braided cord creates a strong accent.

might be affixing to your gift, but it also stands alone as an attractive natural wrapping. Raffia also comes dyed in a range of eye-popping colors. For full raffia bows, you must loop many strands together and tie them in the middle. Cut through the loop on each end, for a frivolous fringed look. Raffia can also be twisted, braided, or shredded into smaller strips.

Organza. This gossamer ribbon shimmers with reflected light. So whispery thin, organza allows whatever it covers to show through. In pastels, organza seems almost celestial, while in richer autumnal hues, the ribbon can imitate a sultan's treasure trove. Organza ribbon easily ties into bows, or can be tied in a simple knot. The cut ends will remain stiff if they are cut short enough. Do keep in mind that organza ribbon ends will ravel, so cut on a diagonal or cut a "V" into the end of the ribbon, also known as a "fishtail".

Wire-edged Ribbon. Manufacturers weave a fine wire along both edges of a ribbon as it is being created. The thin flexible wire enables the ribbon to hold its shape and be looped into bows which hold their form.

Sheer ribbon, especially organza, provides a delicacy unlike any other material. Match or contrast the ribbon to your wrapping, choosing from a vast array of hues.

Cord. Glossy braided or twisted cord, sometimes with a tassel on the end, works well in place of a ribbon, or in conjunction with it. The look is plush and velvety and is a good addition to smaller packages. Cord comes in various thicknesses and is sold in fabric stores and craft-supply shops.

String. String, twine, rope—the old industrial standby for holding goods together and wrapping postal packages—is also a great addition to gift wrapping. Each has its own rugged, rustic look, and when matched with the right paper or gift box (think naturals), string and its relatives can be counted on as alternatives to fancy store-bought ribbon.

Satin. Shiny satin bows come in an array of cheerful colors, and, often, with prints, such as polka-dots, stripes, checks, floral, and much more. A printed satin ribbon on plain paper is often all you need. You can find single-face satin ribbon which bears just one shiny side, or double-faced, which will be shiny on both sides—perfect for making elaborate bows and rosettes.

Velvet. This sumptuous material, with a plush texture and densely woven pile, is the classic ribbon from days of yore. Tie a richly colored velvet ribbon to a simply-wrapped gift and the "elegance quotient" automatically triples.

Scarves. Perhaps untraditional, scarves of silk, tulle, cotton, chiffon, or even wool make alternative "ribbons". Scout through your closet and pull out the most colorful scarves which you never wear, or hunt through a flea market or second-hand store for a handful of inexpensive neck-scarves. Depending on the size of your gift, gather the diagonal ends of a scarf together and twist or fold them, creating a long piece of "ribbon" with which to work. Tie it around the container as you would a normal wide ribbon. Tie the ends in a bow, or fluff the ends after tying them in a knot.

Scarves and antique handkerchiefs are a surprisingly convenient and attractive way of wrapping small gifts.

Tulle. Easily available from a fabric shop or department store, tulle acts as a festive and feminine alternative to ribbon. Cut long strips of the netting and fold or twist them, then tie them around your gift container. Fluff the ends into a fan-shape. Affix another bow to the center of the tie, or perhaps some fabric flowers. Try another idea altogether: use the tulle as your wrapping. First wrap your gift in a sheet of plain colored paper, then pull the tulle up from the bottom of the container, gathering it around the top of the box, and tie a contrasting color of ribbon around it. The colored paper will peek through the tulle netting. Talk about versatile wrapping material!

THE EMBELLISHMENTS

Truly anything can be an embellishment. Depending on the gift, or perhaps the theme of the holiday or occasion, you can add a number of items to the top of your giftwrap for a memorable gift experience.

The Hint—If you have wrapped a teapot or a tea set, why not add some brightly packaged tea bags to the top of the package? Use them instead of a bow, or perhaps peeking out from the loop of the bow. If the gift is a garden tool or garden-related, place a colorful packet of seeds on top, or tie it to the ribbon.

Nut and Dried Fruits—These add a delightful lively spirit to the decor. Be sure your fruits are fully dried, especially if the packages will be lying in wait for a while, such as under a Christmas tree. Ideally your gifts will be exceptionally wrapped so that folks will want to have them under their tree as part of the decoration. Fruits, nuts, cinnamon sticks, all artfully arranged in a garland or attached to a ribbon, can hint at Victorian style, rustic country, or other genres.

Found Objects—Buttons, beads, old jewelry—any number of things can be great gift toppers. Tie beads or old earrings to your ribbon, or simply arrange them in an interesting pattern and glue them to the top. This is also a great way to clean out your jewelry box of unwanted brick-a-brack.

Objects found in nature make the most enchanting enhancements to even the plainest packages. Dried pods, twigs, shells, even a scavenged crab's claw, provide intriguing decorations. Collages, created from your treasures, can be removed and saved.

Natural Items—Leaves, dried flowers, pressed or fresh flowers, twigs, feathers, pods, grasses, and so many other wonderful objects from nature may be used to adorn a gift package. Gathering the stuff is half the fun. Spend a few hours taking a walk in the woods and see how many fascinating decorative bits and pieces you can come up with. Many objects are ready for use, while others may need to be dried. Spread them out on a paper towel in a dry and ventilated area. The sun will bleach them, so keep them in a fairly dark place. Keep a collection on hand, and use a sprig here or there when you have something to wrap.

GIFT TAGS

Gift tags can also be great decorative elements on your package. They enable you to write a sentiment or a nice thought, as well as to identify who the gift is from. When you have gathered all of your materials, make several tags at once. That way, all you

have to do is grab one when the need arises. Tags can be as simple as folded pieces of decorative paper, or more elaborate (like our gift tags on pages 124–125). Stamp your gift tag with decorative designs cut into a potato-half, like you learned to do in grade school. Store-bought stamps have become especially elaborate. You can also create tags with materials other than paper. Write or paint your message on a flat wooden tree ornament, for example. Invent a unique style for your tags, and make lots of them. Your friends will automatically recognize the gift from your special tag.

A stunning gift tag on the top of your package may be all you need in the way of ornamentation.

ADHESIVES

Tape. Use invisible cellophane tape or double-sided invisible cellophane tape.

Craft Glue or PVA. This fast-drying white glue is transparent when dry. Use craft glue for affixing light materials, such as paper decorations, twine, or ribbon to the box (to keep it from slipping), and other small decorative bits to your paper.

Glue Gun and Glue Sticks. The glue gun is *the* crafter's tool. It will help you immensely in gluing down larger decorations. Heavy as well as light objects will benefit in being affixed by this adhesive, since the hot melted glue, dispensed at the squeeze of a trigger, dries instantly and is incredibly strong. Use a glue gun for adhering environmental objects to the tops of gifts, or for gluing several layers of bows onto a box.

CUTTING TOOLS

Scissors. Keep a variety of scissors on hand. Not only will you be cutting paper, you will also cut ribbon, (sometimes with wire in it), fabric, twine, rope, and wire. Keep a set of pinking shears for evening up fabric and keeping it from raveling, as well as for cutting decorative edges. If your organza ribbon, for example, begins to ravel you will need small, sharp scissors to clip the slippery strings. Keep your scissors sharpened and rust-free.

Craft Knife. Craft knives can help you with precise detailing. Use the sharp edge for cutting tags, or for cutting out uneven or curved paper images to use in your decorating. Replace your blades often.

OTHER HELPFUL TOOLS

Glue Brush. When gluing materials together, a glue brush helps to evenly distribute the glue over an area. It will prevent the paper from buckling and warping.

Cutting Mat. When using a craft knife, work on a cutting mat to ensure that you won't accidently slice through other papers with which you are working.

Bone Folder. This tool, which is used in bookmaking, has an end with a point and one rounded end. It, and any other scoring tool, such as a butter knife or corner of a wooden ruler, can be used for making creases in heavy paper. The side of the tool (or you can substitute the back of a spoon) is used for *burnishing* or smoothing out any lumps or air bubbles in your just-glued paper by rubbing over the paper in a circular motion from the center to the edges.

HOW TO...

1. Place your gift box on the sheet of wrapping paper you intend to use. Measure the paper to fit your box. The ends of the paper should be at least half the height of the box, plus 1 inch (2.5 cm). The width of the paper should wrap around the box with ½ inch (1.3 cm) extra for an overlap. Cut your paper accordingly.

2. Wrap the paper tightly around the gift, and tape the edge of the first flap of paper to the box to keep the paper from sliding around. If you are using paper with a pattern, be sure the paper lines up to create one uninterrupted pattern.

3. Bring the other side of the wrapping paper over the box and fold the edge under, so it creates a neatly creased edge. Tape this down. (Use double-sided tape and tape the paper on the underside, for the most attractive results.)

4. Fold over the top edge of the paper on the ends of the box and tape it to the box with double-sided tape.

5. Crease the side flaps into the corners and crease the edge of the bottom flap inward to create a neat, folded edge.

6. Bring the bottom flap up and tape.

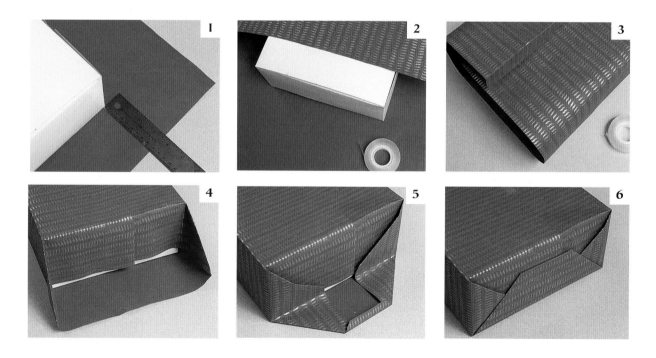

HOW TO...

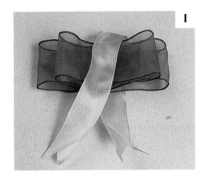

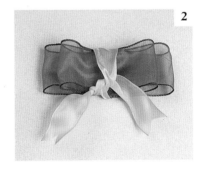

DOUBLE BOW

1. Cut a 12-inch (30 cm) piece of ribbon. Fold it down to form a loop, with the two ends overlapping in the back. Cut another length of ribbon about 2 inches (5 cm) smaller. Place the second ribbon on top of the first. Cut another piece of ribbon the same size as the second piece and fold it over the two loops, from back to front.

2. Tie the third ribbon around the two loops into a knot. Pull it tight and slide the knot around to the back.

3. Cut each end of the dangling ribbon into a "V", or "fishtail." Fluff the loops outward. (See finished bow above.)

4. Secure the bow to your gift with hot glue or tape, or string a piece of wire or thread through the knot in the back, and tie it to a ribbon on the package.

VARIATION:

Festoon an old brooch or button to the center of the bow for a more elaborate look. We found these gems at a flea-market.

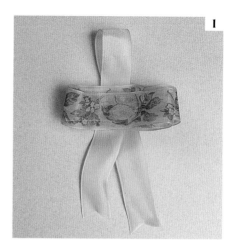

CROSSED BOW

1. Cut two 12-inch (30 cm) pieces of ribbon. Fold them into loops, with the two ends overlapping in the back. Place the loops on top of each other. Cut a piece of ribbon 14 inches (35 cm) long. Fold the longer ribbon in half behind the two loops.

2. Cut two pieces of thin ribbon the same length. Lay them across the other bow loops to form an X as shown.

3. Tie the thin ribbons one at a time at the back of the bow. (The bow will look crooked after tying the first ribbon, but will be symmetrical when both are tied.) Leave the thin ribbon uncut, so that you may use the ends to secure the bow to the gift.

4. Cut the long ends of the ribbon into a "V". (See finished bow above.)

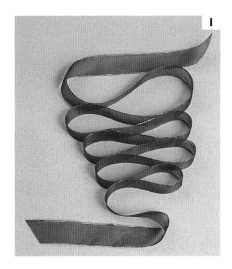

MULTI-BOW

1. Cut a long piece of ribbon, approximately 36 inches (90 cm) long. Zigzag the ribbon into loops, making the loops longer at the top and narrower at the bottom.

2. Bring the loops together and tie them in the middle with a piece of thin gold wire ribbon or gold cord. Move the knot to the back of the bow.

3. Pull the loops out, so that each loop is visible. Trim the tails to equal length. (See finished bow above.)

GIFTWRAPPING TIPS

❖ Enhance large boxes by using crepe paper streamers as ribbon. That way you won't have to spend oodles on expensive ribbons.

❖ Don't be sparing with tape. To create crease-free wrapping without bulges or buckling and to ensure that sharp corners stay that way, tape after every fold. Use double-sided cellophane tape for the best results.

❖ Save old greeting cards and cut them into shapes to paste onto a package as part of the decoration. Color coordinate the paper and card pieces for a catchy mix of prints.

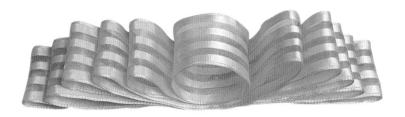

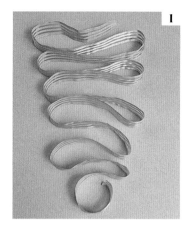

STACKED BOW

1. Cut a long piece of ribbon, approximately 36 inches (90 cm) long. Zigzag the ribbon into loops, making the loops longer at the top and narrower at the bottom.

2. Gather the loops together and tape them in the middle. Curl the short end into a circle and tape it at the bottom, so that the circle stays. (You may want to pin it in the middle with a straight pin, pinning from the bottom of the bow.)

3. Tape or hot glue the finished bow onto your gift.

DOUBLE BOW

1. Cut two ribbons the same length. Zigzag the first ribbon and place the second ribbon on top of the first, also looped back and forth, from right to left.

2. Gather the ribbon loops together flat, and tie a thin gold wire ribbon or gold cord around the middle.

3. Push the knotted gold ribbon to the back of the bow and fluff the loops so that they form a circular shape. (See finished bow above.)

Tip: Longer ribbon and more loops will create a fuller, rounder bow.

SHOELACE BOW

1. Cut a long piece of wired ribbon. Cut the ends into a "fishtail."

2. Make a loop out of the left end of the ribbon, leaving a tail, and loop the right side underneath the ribbon and back over the top again.

3. Slip a loop from the right side of the ribbon through the folded-over part of the ribbon.

4. Pull the loop through the knot completely, and make sure that both sides are even. Fluff the bow.

Who gives me, teaches me to give. –Dutch Proverb

GIFTWRAP PROJECTS

ORGANZA AND BEADS

DESIGNER: CONSTANCE ENSNER

*T*his striking presentation combines elegant ribbon and beads with a simple box, creating a sleek and modern design. Salvage your broken costume jewelry for beads, buttons, and baubles.

YOU WILL NEED

- ❖ Natural cardboard box
- ❖ Organza ribbon
- ❖ Thin copper wire
- ❖ Beads from broken necklaces or bracelets
- ❖ Scissors or deckle-edged scissors
- ❖ Wire cutter

Tip: Do you have a stash of broken jewelry, buttons, beads, and baubles? These items can add a quick decorative touch to any present and can be easily adapted to the size of your package.

INSTRUCTIONS

1. Since your gift box may vary in size, measure your ribbon around the box before cutting it. Make sure the ribbon meets at the top of the box, and add 2 inches (5 cm) to either end.

2. Cut strips of the organza ribbon, either with regular or deckled scissors. Tie four strips (or more, depending on the size of your box) of the ribbon into a knot at the top of the box, spacing them about ½ inch (1.3 cm) apart.

3. With wire cutters, trim at least 4 inches (10 cm) of the thin copper wire for each ribbon. Thread your first bead (in this case, the crystal bead), and twist the wire into a small knot at the top opening of the bead. Trim off the excess wire so only the knot remains.

4. Thread the next bead, which should be a bit wider than the first. Pull the free end of the wire around the knot in the organza ribbon, twisting the copper wire back around itself, and trim off the excess. Make sure the beads fit snugly against the ribbon and that their weight doesn't cause them to wobble around on the box.

5. Repeat these steps for each of the ribbons on the box.

NATURAL GRASS AND POD WRAP

DESIGNER: NICOLE TUGGLE

*T*his wrapping combines varied textures of handmade paper and natural colors to create a sophisticated foundation for a gracefully long bundle of dried grasses and flower pods.

YOU WILL NEED

- ❖ 1 large sheet of hand-made paper in a natural shade
- ❖ Sheet of light green decorative paper with smooth texture
- ❖ Sheet of heavy stock paper in coordinating color
- ❖ Bundle of dried grasses, longer than the box you are wrapping
- ❖ Sheer organza ribbon
- ❖ Glue gun and glue sticks
- ❖ Tape
- ❖ Scissors

VARIATION

If you can't find long grasses, stems of eucalyptus, live branches of a fern plant, and long-stemmed dried flowers also make attractive bundles.

INSTRUCTIONS

1. Cut the paper to fit your gift box. Using the large sheet of handmade paper, wrap your gift box as usual. Because this paper will be thicker than regular wrapping paper, tape may not hold it together, in which case you may glue the end flaps to the covered part of the box ends. Rest the box on each glued side for several minutes to allow the glue to set.

2. Cut the sheet of green decorative paper lengthwise so it is narrower than the box. (**Tip:** For an accurate fit, measure 2 inches (5 cm) in from the sides of the box, and cut the paper to fit within those measurements.)

3. Wrap the strip of decorative paper around the box, concealing the folded edges of the handmade paper. Use cellophane tape to fasten one edge of the paper strip over the other edge underneath the box.

4. Tie the stems of the dried flower pods and the ends of the bundle of long grasses together with sheer organza ribbon, wrapping the ribbon around them several times and tying it off. Cut the ends off near the knot.

5. Placing the bundle with the knotted side down, deposit a dot of hot glue on the wrapped ribbon, and angle the bundle diagonally across the gift box. Press the bundle down onto the narrow strip of decorative paper at the glued spot. (Tip: Use the glue sparingly and the bundle may be taken off the package and saved later.)

6. Cut a square out of a piece of heavy stock paper in a coordinating color for your gift tag. Sign it, and slide it under the edge of the dried grass bouquet.

SUPER SUNFLOWER WRAP

DESIGNER: TRACI NEIL-TAYLOR

*R*epeat the theme of snazzy commercial paper as part of the decoration for an extra-splashy presentation. Note the charming touch of the hand-stamped gift tag and a packet of seeds.

YOU WILL NEED

- ❖ Commercial wrapping paper with sunflower print
- ❖ 1-inch-wide (2.5 cm) grosgrain ribbon, bright yellow
- ❖ 2-inch-wide (5 cm) grosgrain ribbon, dark yellow
- ❖ 3 silk leaves
- ❖ 3 silk sunflowers
- ❖ Piece of card stock
- ❖ Stamp
- ❖ Ink pad
- ❖ Bundle of lavender
- ❖ Packet of sunflower seeds
- ❖ Craft glue
- ❖ Tape
- ❖ Scissors
- ❖ Deckle-edged scissors

VARIATION

Hand-letter and draw your sunflower card with a gold pen, rather than using a stamp.

INSTRUCTIONS

1. Wrap your gift item in a box as usual, using the brightly printed sunflower paper.

2. Wrap the bright yellow ribbon around the box and tie a simple knot, leaving 4-inch-long (10 cm) tails on each end of the ribbon. Cut the ends in a "fishtail."

3. Cut another piece of the bright yellow ribbon, 8 inches (20 cm) long. Tie it in a knot around the knot of the first ribbon. Cut the ends in a "fishtail."

4. Cut the dark yellow wider ribbon into a 10-inch-long (25 cm) strip. Tie it around the two knots in the center of the package, and cut a "fishtail" into the ends.

5. Place a spot of craft glue onto the base of the silk leaves. Press them down around the ribbons, leaving enough room for the silk flowers.

6. Place a dot of glue onto the bottom of the silk blossoms and nestle them over the leaves, close to the central knot of tied ribbons.

7. While the glued leaves and flowers are drying, cut a square out of the card stock with deckle-edged scissors.

8. Using a sunflower stamp and ink pad, stamp an impression onto the center of the card.

9. Slip the lavender bundle under the ribbon that surrounds the box.

10. Tape the stamped card under the edge of the bundle.

11. Tuck a packet of sunflower seeds into the center decoration.

CANDY WRAPPERS

DESIGNER: TRACI NEIL-TAYLOR

*A*s bright and colorful as tasty sweets, these "candy" packages brighten any birthday table. Use tissue or crepe paper and sheathe it in opalescent cellophane. Tie off the ends with fancy silk or foil ribbon for extra pizzazz.

YOU WILL NEED

❖ Tissue or crepe paper, bright colors
❖ Cellophane paper
❖ Ribbon, ⅛ to ½ inch (3 mm to 1.3 cm) wide
❖ Postal cylinder tube
❖ Tape
❖ Scissors
❖ Deckle-edged scissors

INSTRUCTIONS

1. Cut pieces of tissue or crepe paper and cellophane equal in size for the same package. Be sure that the paper extends 2 or 3 inches (5 or 7.5 cm) beyond the ends of the postal tube.

2. Wrap the tube in the tissue or crepe paper first.

3. Cover the wrapped tube with the cellophane paper.

4. Gather and tie the ends off with ribbon.

5. Cut the ends of the ribbon to the same length.

6. Cut the ends of the paper with the deckled scissors, making sure the ends are the same length.

VARIATIONS

Wrap a box completely with your base paper, taping the ends down as usual. Cover the container with cellophane paper, gathering the excess paper at the ends and tying them off with ribbon, as you would the cylindrical packages.

Use printed paper as your base, and match the ribbon to a predominant color in the wrapping.

ENVIRONMENTAL ART WRAPS

DESIGNER: CAROL STANGLER

Spend an afternoon in the woods or your garden scouring the ground for twigs, seed pods, feathers, and other natural materials. Just these few gentle elements, artfully placed, provide an expression of simple beauty which only the earth's treasures can convey

YOU WILL NEED

- ❖ Brown paper bags
- ❖ Twine or cord made of natural fiber
- ❖ Found natural objects, i.e., dried plant material, feathers, seedpods, twigs, etc.
- ❖ Tape
- ❖ Glue gun and glue sticks
- ❖ Scissors

Tip: Always be on the alert for a knobby twig, a twisted pod, or an unusually smooth stone. Gather objects which vary in texture and form, and which delight you in general. Keep them stored in a dark, dry area, and refer back to them when gift-giving occasions arise.

Vertical Wraps

INSTRUCTIONS

1. Cut open a brown paper bag, and wrap your gift box as usual.

2. Triple tie the package with twine or cordage.

3. Place the natural materials vertically in an attractive arrangement, and space them apart equally across the front of the box. Insert the stems through the twine, weaving the stems over the first strand of twine, under the middle strand, and over the bottom strand.

4. With the glue gun, place a dot of glue onto the package where the stem meets the paper underneath the twine or at the bottom portion of the stem closer to the edge of the package, and press the stem into the glue lightly. This will keep the elements from sliding.

5. If you have gathered material without stems, such as flat leaves, dried flower heads, or bark, place a dot of glue on the back side of these objects and press them lightly onto the package.

Collage Wrap

INSTRUCTIONS

1. Create a collage of natural plant materials first, by hot gluing each element onto a wide base, such as a piece of birch bark. Allow this to dry.

2. Glue the collage diagonally onto the brown paper-wrapped box.

3. Carefully tie a piece of cord around the package, and anchor the knot at the base of the collage. Cut off the long ends of the cord.

4. Tuck one last element into the knot to complete the collage.

CRACKERS

Designer: Nancy Worrell

*I*deal for hiding little promissory notes, gift coupons, money, and more, "crackers" are also ideal party favors. An English Christmas tradition, crackers are stuffed with a note of good cheer or good fortune. After Christmas dinner, when the crackers are opened by pulling on both sides simultaneously, they make a delightful pop.

METALLIC STARS CRACKER

INSTRUCTIONS

1. Trim the edges of the paper with your decorative-edged scissors.

2. Sponge print stars on corrugated cardboard with gold and silver metallic paints, and allow the stars to dry.

YOU WILL NEED

- ❖ 1 piece of corrugated cardboard, blue
- ❖ Acrylic paint, gold and silver metallics
- ❖ Sponge cut into star shape
- ❖ Gold and silver paper, the same size as the corrugated paper
- ❖ Decorative scissors with pinking edge
- ❖ Craft glue
- ❖ Scissors

3. Cut gold and silver papers down the middle from either end of the cracker. Position the silver paper along the inside edge of the corrugated paper with the right side of the silver paper to the inside (wrong side) of the corrugated paper, and glue it. Position the gold paper on top of the silver paper with wrong sides together. Glue this and allow the glue to dry. Repeat for the other end.

4. Roll up the corrugated paper with your gift positioned in the center. Glue along the edge of the paper.

5. Cut the gold and silver papers into ¼-inch (6 mm) strips to the edge of the corrugated paper. Using your scissors' edge, carefully curl the paper ends.

CHECKERBOARD CRACKER

INSTRUCTIONS

1. Measure and cut the silver paper large enough to cover the tube with an approximate ½-inch (1.3 cm) extension on either end. Mark a ½-inch (1.3 cm) border around the edge of the silver paper. Measure and mark approximately half of the lines one way between the borders. Using a craft knife, cut slits in the paper between the marked borders.

YOU WILL NEED

- ❖ Paper tube
- ❖ 1 piece of silver paper large enough to cover the tube
- ❖ 1 sheet each of blue/turquoise and green/lime colored paper
- ❖ Craft knife and cutting mat
- ❖ Metal ruler
- ❖ Corkboard or clipboard
- ❖ Craft glue
- ❖ Scissors

2. Cut the colored papers into ½-inch (1.3 cm) strips, twice the width of the silver paper.

3. Pin the silver paper on the corkboard or clip on the clipboard with cuts going up and down. Weave the colored paper strips with silver paper, alternating colors, as shown here. Adjust the colored papers so that they are even on both sides of the silver paper.

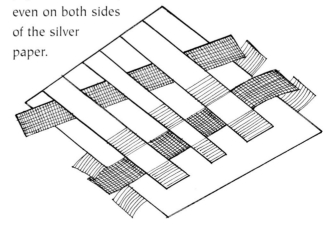

4. Cover the tube with the woven paper and glue.

5. Cut the colored paper ends into ¼-inch (6mm) strips to the edge of the silver paper. Using your scissors' edge, carefully curl the paper ends.

GOLD AND RED CRACKER

INSTRUCTIONS

1. Roll the corrugated paper into a tube, and glue along edge.

2. Center the doily, and glue it to the rolled paper. Tie it with raffia and the gold ribbon, and stick a sprig of baby's breath in the bow.

3. Dab gold metallic paint onto tissue paper. Allow it to dry. Cut the paper in half and stuff it in either end of roll.

> YOU WILL NEED
> ❖ 1 piece of corrugated paper, red
> ❖ Gold paper doily
> ❖ 3 yards (2.7 m) raffia
> ❖ 1 yard (.9 m) gold ribbon, ¼ inch (6mm) wide
> ❖ Sprig of baby's breath
> ❖ Craft glue
> ❖ 1 sheet of white tissue paper (optional)
> ❖ Acrylic paint, gold metallic (optional)

PAPER POCKETS

DESIGNER: NANCY WORRELL

*T*hese charming little paper pockets are ideal for wrapping small items. They are so simple to make, and require few manterials. Make several at once, and keep them on hand for those special gift treasures.

> YOU WILL NEED
> ❖ Handmade paper
> ❖ Craft glue
> ❖ 3-inch (7.5 cm) piece of gold ribbon, ¼ inch (6 mm) wide
> ❖ Sealing wax and stamp

Pocket 1

INSTRUCTIONS

1. Cut a 3 x 12 inch (7.5 x 30 cm) piece of handmade paper.

2. With the paper in front of you and beginning at the bottom

right corner, fold the corner up and align it with the top edge of the paper. Fold over the aligning folded edge with the bottom of the paper. Glue the folded edge to the bottom edge of the paper.

3. With the paper in front of you, fold the left corner down to align with the bottom edge of the paper. Tuck the end of the left fold into the right fold to form a pocket, and glue the papers together at this point.

4. Position the folded ribbon on the pocket where the edges overlap. Secure the ribbon and overlapping edges with sealing wax. Stamp a design into the sealing wax.

Pocket 2

INSTRUCTIONS

1. Cut a piece of kraft paper, 3 x 12 inches (7.5 x 30 cm). Trim the edges with decorative scissors.

2. With the paper in front of you and beginning at the bottom right corner, fold the corner up, and align it with the top edge of the paper. Fold it over, aligning the folded edge with the bottom of the paper. Glue the folded edge to the bottom edge of the paper.

3. Fold the doily in half. Align the edge of the folded doily with the left edge of the kraft paper, placing the kraft paper inside of the folded doily.

4. With the paper in front of you, fold the left corner down to align with the bottom edge of the paper. Fold the doily with the paper. Tuck the end of the left fold into right fold to form a pocket and glue them together.

5. Thread a gold wire ribbon through the button and tie the ribbon. Glue the button with the ribbon to the paper pocket. Twist the ribbon into a curly-cue.

YOU WILL NEED
❖ Kraft paper
❖ 8-inch (20 cm) white paper lace doily
❖ Gold wire ribbon, ¼-inch (6 mm) wide
❖ White decorative button
❖ Craft glue
❖ Decorative scissors with scallop edge

Tip: Select the correct weight of paper for your package. It's difficult to wrap a very small pacakge in heavy paper, for example. If you are planning to glue decorations onto your wrapped gift, the paper shouldn't be so thin that a glued object might rip the paper by its weight alone.

WINE AND ROSES

DESIGNER: MOLLY SIEBURG

*F*resh flowers are some of nature's most beautiful decorations. A gift doesn't always have to be wrapped or covered, in the traditional manner. A gift can easily be nestled amongst a floral bouquet. This is a perfect house gift or romantic present— complete with a chilled bottle of wine, flower/wine bucket, and delicate blossoms, so pleasing to the eye.

INSTRUCTIONS

1. Cut a piece of floral foam to fit into the bottom of the bucket. It will elevate the wine bottle, so that it peeks out from the flowers.

YOU WILL NEED
- ❖ French flower bucket
- ❖ Wine bottle
- ❖ Floral foam
- ❖ Fresh flowers
- ❖ Galax leaves or other greenery
- ❖ Scissors, or flower cutting shears

2. Fill the bucket halfway with water.

3. Measure how long the stems of your flowers should be, so that the heads will peek out over the rim of the bucket.

4. Cut the stems, including roses.

5. Arrange the flowers around the wine bottle so that they create a ring around the bottle. The flowers should be dense enough so that they hold each other up and spill over the rim slightly.

6. Incorporate galax leaves or other greenery into the bouquet at intervals.

The Meaning of Flowers

The flower became so adored by the people of the Victorian Era that in 1879 an entire book by Miss Corruthers of Inverness was dedicated to the language of flowers. This book became the standard source for flower symbolism both in England and the United States. The flower afforded a silent language, especially for lovers, that allowed them to communicate many sentiments that the propriety of the times would not normally allow. Today, we still retain some of that symbolism for certain flowers.

Classical Victorian Meanings of Flowers
Amaryllis - Beautiful but timid
Anemone - Forsaken
Aster - Variety
Buttercup - Riches
Camellia - Gratitude
Carnation - Pure and deep love
Chrysanthemum - A desolate heart
Dahlia - Dignity and elegance
Daffodil - Unrequited love
Daisy - I will think about it
Forget-me-not - Do not forget
Geranium - I prefer you
Hibiscus - Delicate beauty
Holly - Am I forgotten
Hyacinth - Constancy
Iris - A message for thee
Jonquil - Desire
Purple Lilac - First emotions of love
White Lilac - Youth
Lily of the Valley - Return of happiness
Marigold - Sacred affection
Morning Glory - Affection
Poppy - Consolation
Red Rose - I love you
White Rose - Silence
Wild Rose - Simplicity
Yellow Rose - Unfaithfulness
Violet - Faithfulness
Zinnia - I mourn your absence

FRESH LEAF WRAPS

DESIGNER: MOLLY SIEBURG

Wrapping with fresh leaves requires only a large plant, or a floral shop that usually keeps big decorative leaves on hand. The dark, deeply veined leaves make a stunning jewelry box wrapping, or a wrap for something extra special. Bear in mind that the leaves will begin to wilt after several hours, so tell your delighted friend to open the present as soon as possible.

YOU WILL NEED

- ❖ Peace lily leaves (or leaves from any large plant)
- ❖ Caladium leaves (or any smaller leaves)
- ❖ Ornamental grasses
- ❖ Tape or spray adhesive
- ❖ Wire (optional)

Tips: Smaller boxes will require fewer or smaller leaves.

Ornamental grasses wrapped around other leaves provide variation in color and texture.

INSTRUCTIONS

1. For the larger box, you will need about four leaves to cover the surface. Wrap one leaf around each end and attach it to the package with tape or spray adhesive.

2. Wrap a large leaf around the bottom of the box, and tape or glue it to the top.

3. Wrap the last leaf around the front of the box, and tape or glue it to the back.

4. Make "bows" out of the leaves by folding over the leaves, tip to stem. Secure them with tape or a small piece of wire.

5. Layer three or four leaves on top of one another for a three-dimensional effect, and tape or glue them to the top of the box.

FANCY PLACE MAT WRAP

DESIGNER: VADIM BORA

If you're hunting for a quick and inventive giftwrap, look in your dining room drawer. Place mats easily conform to the shape of a bottle. Tie a ribbon around the middle and this house gift is good to go. So simple, yet smashing!

YOU WILL NEED

❖ Clean place mats
❖ Wire ribbon
❖ Raffia, gold
❖ Twisted paper ribbon
❖ Deckle-edged scissors

India Red and Gold Mat

INSTRUCTIONS

1. Wrap a long strand of gold raffia around the neck of your gift bottle. Tie it in a knot at the neck, but leave one end of the raffia as long as the bottle itself.

2. Place your gift bottle on its side on the edge of a place mat with the bottom of the bottle even with the bottom edge of the mat.

3. Roll the bottle with the mat until the fabric reaches all the way around. Be sure to leave the long strand of raffia out of the wrapping.

4. With the wrapped bottle still lying down, wrap a piece of wire ribbon around the middle of the bottle. Twist it closed in back.

5. Wrap a long strand of raffia around the middle of the wide wire ribbon three or four times and tie it off in the back.

6. Place the long strand of raffia that you earlier tied around the neck of the bottle over the top edge of the place mat so that it hangs down in front of the bottle.

Bamboo Mat

1. Wrap the bottle with a bamboo place mat as described above.

2. Use a long piece of twisted paper ribbon to wrap around the middle of the wrapped bottle several times.

3. Unfurl one end of the twisted paper ribbon and cut the tip with deckle-edged scissors.

4. Tie the end of the ribbon as if you were tying a bow, but only bring one end through.

PROSPERITY WRAPPING

DESIGNER: PEI-LING BECKER

*A*pparent in this exquisite wrapping is the Asian influence of harmony, preciseness, and distinctive elements combined to work as a whole. Note the addition of the small paper fan, which represents prosperity in Asia. Some unfamiliar items, such as the gold-striped Mizuhiki wire and the patterned origami paper, add an exotic surprise.

YOU WILL NEED

- Commercial wrapping paper or origami paper
- Textured decorative paper, red and white
- Gold foil paper
- Gold elastic string
- Red elastic tie
- Beads on wire
- Wire
- Mizuhiki paper cord (available at craft-supply stores or Asian markets)
- Craft glue
- Scissors
- Wire cutters (optional)

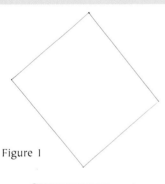

Figure 1

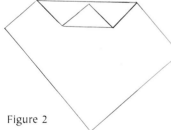

Figure 2

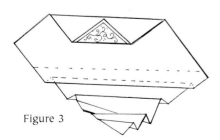

Figure 3

INSTRUCTIONS

1. Cut a strip of wrapping paper or origami paper narrower than the box. Wrap the box so that the edges show evenly on either side.

2. Tie a gold elastic string diagonally around two corners of the box.

3. Fold the white textured paper following figures 1 through 4. (Glue a piece of decorative paper onto the folded tip created after figure 2.)

4. Make a fold in a small piece of the red paper, and glue it onto the center strip of the white paper.

5. Make a tiny fan by folding the gold foil paper neatly into evenly spaced vertical strips. Twist a small piece of wire around the base of the fan and clip it off close to the base. Loop the red elastic string around the base of the fan.

6. Twist the Mizuhiki paper cord into a double circle, but allow the ends to protrude past the intersection where they cross. Using regular wire, tie the intersection of the Mizuhiki cord so they won't slip. Take six more wires and tie them in a knot at the base of the circle. Using your regular wire, tie the small circle into place where the Mizuhiki cord ends cross. Add the beads on wire under the thin wire tie.

7. Wrap four pieces of Mizuhiki cord of a different color combination around the white paper rectangle and secure them with wire on the underside.

8. Arrange the components on the center of the white paper and glue them down. Glue the entire decoration into the center of the gift.

VARIATIONS

Attach other small folded pieces of decorative paper. Experiment with a number of shapes, and glue them on at random.

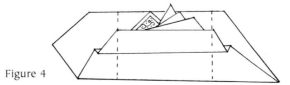

Figure 4

FOLDED BOXES

DESIGNER: NANCY WORRELL

*E*ver so elegant, these charming little containers can harbor a number of treasures inside—from pearls and cuff links, to an engagement ring or a deluxe chocolate truffle. Once you learn to make the basic box, you may embellish at will, decorating for each particular occasion. You may wish to present a collection of the boxes in complementary designs and colors to one person. Later, they may be used as a tabletop decoration or part of a centerpiece.

White Box

INSTRUCTIONS

1. Create a watercolor wash on the paper using diluted watercolors. Allow this to dry. Spray or paint the paper with gold glitter mist.

2. Use the pattern (on page 53) to cut the box from the watercolor paper. Trim the edges with decorative scissors.

3. Referring to your pattern, fold the box, scoring the lines as needed. Fasten the ends by sliding them into the cut slots.

4. Glue the silk flower to one point of the box top.

YOU WILL NEED

❖ One 9 in. x 12 in. (22.5 x 30 cm) sheet of heavy watercolor paper

❖ Watercolors, red and blue

❖ Gold glitter mist (optional)

❖ Craft glue

❖ White silk flower

❖ Deckle-edged scissors

❖ Scoring tool

Gray Striped Box

YOU WILL NEED
- ❖ One sheet of gray paper 150 g/m²
- ❖ Watercolors
- ❖ Straightedge ruler
- ❖ Silver leafing pen
- ❖ Copper leafing pen
- ❖ Scoring tool

INSTRUCTIONS

1. Use the pattern to cut a box from the paper.

2. Use the straightedge ruler and leafing pens to draw a striped pattern from point to point of the box.

3. Referring to the pattern, fold the box, scoring the lines as needed. Fasten the ends by sliding into the cut slots.

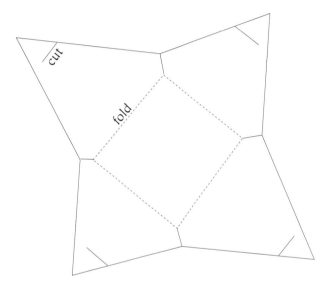

Music Memories Box

YOU WILL NEED
- ❖ Sheet music
- ❖ Matte interior varnish
- ❖ Crackle finish
- ❖ Acrylic paint, metallic gold, diluted
- ❖ Gold leafing pen
- ❖ 1 small gold button
- ❖ 1 red tassel, 1 inch (2.5 cm)
- ❖ Craft glue
- ❖ Paint brush

INSTRUCTIONS

1. Seal both sides of the sheet music with varnish. Allow this to dry.

2. Following the manufacturer's directions, apply the crackle finish.

3. Use a paper towel to dab gold paint onto the paper and rub off, highlighting the crackle finish. Allow it to dry.

4. Use the pattern to cut your box from the crackled sheet music.

5. Use the leafing pen to draw a gold border around the outside edge of the box.

6. Referring to the pattern, fold the box, scoring the lines as needed. Fasten the ends by sliding them into the cut slots.

7. Glue the tassel and button to one point on the box.

DIAPHANOUS BOTTLE WRAPPINGS

DESIGNER: CORINNE KURZMANN

*W*hen giving homemade gifts of bottled vinegars or oils, why cover over the beautiful *contents? Gorgeous organza ribbon creates a translucent ornamentation, allowing the peppers, flowers, herbs, and other elements to shine through.*

YOU WILL NEED

❖ Bottle of herbal vinegar or oil

❖ 1 to 1½ yards (.9 to 1.40 m) of organza ribbon

❖ Garnish (to match contents in bottle)

❖ 12 inches (30 cm) of thick thread

❖ One small bundle of dried lavender

❖ 30 inches (77 cm) of ribbon, ⅛ inch (3 mm) wide

❖ Sewing needle

❖ Scissors

INSTRUCTIONS

1. Gently wrap the bottle three or four times with the organza ribbon, and bring the sides of equal length together.

2. Choose a decorative element that matches or complements the interior contents, to add to the exterior of the bottle. To attach the dried peppers, thread a needle with strong thread and pierce a pepper at its thickest point near the top, but under the stem. Pull the needle and thread through.

3. Tie a knot under the first pepper, and add another pepper to the string, in the same manner, leaving a ½-inch (1.3 cm) length of thread between the two peppers. Tie the knot under the second pepper and string another.

4. Tie off the last knot, and cut the thread.

5. Affix the peppers to the ribbon by tying a knot in the ribbon, placing the thick stem of the first pepper in the middle of that knot.

6. Tie the organza ribbon around the top pepper stem, and wrap the ribbon around the bottle, tying it in back and clipping the ends.

7. For the lavender bundle, take the ⅛-inch-wide (3 mm) ribbon, holding approximately 10 inches (25 cm) in your hand along with the lavender stems. Weave the remaining length of ribbon in and out of the exterior "leaves" of the bundle, leaving ½-inch (1.3 cm) gaps in between.

8. When you reach the top, tuck four thin lavender stems into the top of the bundle and bend them backward over the woven bundle. Weave the remaining ribbon around the single stems. Tie the ribbon into a bow.

9. Tie the organza ribbon around the vinegar bottle, and slide the lavender bundle under the organza ribbon.

LACE PAPER WRAP

DESIGNER: NICOLE TUGGLE

This whispery lacelike paper allows colorful handmade paper to peek through. Japanese ichmatsu paper feels like fabric and comes in various patterns. With a layering of cutout designs that echo the motif in the lace paper, an engaging three-dimensional arrangement emerges.

INSTRUCTIONS

1. Using the large sheet of handmade paper, wrap the gift box as usual. You will need to save scraps of the same paper large enough to cut out the star decorations. If the handmade paper you have chosen is thicker than regular wrapping paper, you may need to affix the folded flaps at the ends of the box with hot glue, rather than tape.

2. Cut a sheet of lace or ichmatsu paper (found in art-supply stores) slightly smaller than the width of the box, and long enough to wrap around the box lengthwise. Save enough for cutting out your decorative pieces later. Carefully wrap the paper around and adhere one end to the bottom of the box with a glue stick. Glue the other end over the top of the first, making sure that the lace paper fits snugly around the box.

(**Tip:** Because the lace paper is quite delicate and absorbent, a glue stick ensures that the paper will not become soggy.

3. Place the raffia around the gift in a T-shape, pulling the ends tightly, and tying them off underneath the box.

4. To create the decoration, look through the scraps of the lace paper you have, and cut out three or four of the star or leaf designs.

5. Place the star or leaf motif on the handmade paper and trace around it, leaving an extra $\frac{1}{8}$ inch (3 mm) showing. Cut the design out of the handmade paper.

6. Lightly dab the back of the lace paper design with a glue stick and adhere it to the handmade paper design, pressing lightly, and smoothing it over with your fingers or the round part of a spoon.

7. Using the glue gun, place a spot of glue onto the back of the handmade paper decoration and press onto the raffia. Do so with two or three more, layering them in a fan shape on top of each other to create a three-dimensional effect.

STACKED AND GILDED HATBOXES

DESIGNER: SUSAN KINNEY

*O*ld hatboxes, found at flea markets or second-hand shops, are covered and revamped into a spectacular stacked package.

INSTRUCTIONS

1. Slightly crumple the burgundy sheets of tissue paper.

2. Spread out the newsprint in a well-ventilated area, and spray each crumpled sheet of tissue with gold spray paint.

3. Cut two strips of gold and burgundy tissue, 3 inches (7.5 cm) wide and the length of the sheet of tissue paper. These strips will be used as the ribbon.

4. Alternate the gold tissue paper and the gilded paper between the boxes and the lids. Wrap the lids and boxes, covering the outside first, and pulling the edges of the paper toward the inside.

5. Glue the tissue to the inside rim of the lid with the glue gun. Do the same with the boxes, gluing the tissue to the interior sides of the box. Cut off any excess paper.

YOU WILL NEED

❖ Three hatboxes, small, medium, and large
❖ Several sheets of tissue paper, in gold and burgundy
❖ Newsprint
❖ Can of gold spray paint
❖ Small dried roses
❖ Glue gun and glue sticks
❖ Scissors

6. Place your gifts into the hatboxes, cushioning them with scraps of crushed tissue paper.

7. Close and stack the boxes. Cross the tissue paper ribbon on a flat surface. Put the stacked boxes over the intersection of the ribbon. Pull the ribbon up over the sides of the boxes, and tie each in a bow at the top.

8. Arrange the small dried roses in a cluster, and glue to the top box beside the bow.

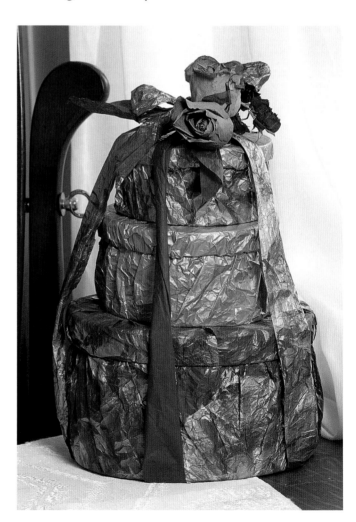

TEA BAG BOW

DESIGNER: MYRNA HARRIGAN

*G*iving a teapot or a tea set as a present? Add to the theme by including a fan of colorful tea bags as the bow.

INSTRUCTIONS

1. Wrap your gift box as usual.

2. Tie wired ribbon around the box on all four sides, leaving the ends long enough to tie in a large shoelace-type bow. (See page 27.)

3. Make two "fans" by stapling five to seven tea bags together at one end.

4. Fold a second piece of ribbon into thirds, forming loop ends. Hold this piece in the middle of the "shoelace" bow on top of the package.

5. Tie the tea bags to the middle of the bow with a piece of thin wire or narrow ribbon.

6. Fluff the ribbon, and cut the loose ends slightly longer than the bow.

YOU WILL NEED

❖ Commercial wrapping paper
❖ Wired ribbon, 1½ inch (3.8 cm) wide
❖ 10 to 14 tea bags
❖ Stapler
❖ A piece of thin-gauge wire or narrow ribbon
❖ Scissors

Tip: For extra fullness, before tying the first "shoelace" bow on top, add a second piece of folded ribbon to the center of the bow.

59

MAP WRAP

DESIGNER: CAROL STANGLER

*W*ith *lines, colors, and symbols, all juxtaposed in one unfolding sheet of paper, maps are the perfect wrapping. Beyond physical travel, however, maps symbolize journeys in spirit. Whether cloaking a gift to an adventurer, a gift celebrating a move or job promotion, a new child or another birthday, maps convey the spiritual equivalent of entering new territory.*

YOU WILL NEED

❖ Maps (road maps, topographical maps, world atlases, etc.)
❖ Ribbon or raffia
❖ Postcard or image from a magazine
❖ Tape
❖ Glue
❖ Glue brush
❖ Scissors

Tip: Are you a traveler? Why not pick up some wrapping paper on your next journey to a foreign land? If you've brought back souvenirs as gifts, wrap them in paper from the country of origin for exotic flavor and an enhancement to the gift.

INSTRUCTIONS

1. Cut the map to fit your box, and wrap the gift as usual.

2. Double or triple wrap ribbon or raffia around your package in two horizontal lines and two vertical lines, evenly spaced apart. Tie off the raffia into a knot, and clip the ends close to the knot.

3. Cut four pieces of matching raffia or ribbon, 3 inches (7.5 cm) long. Tie each of these at the four intersections where the vertical and horizontal strands of raffia meet.

4. Cut a decorative picture or drawing out of a magazine or from a postcard, and center it in between the frame created by the raffia or ribbon.

5. Lightly brush glue along the edges of the picture, and smooth it into place in the center of the package.

VARIATIONS

Instead of using two-dimensional images, thread keys, metro tokens, inexpensive ethnic rings, or other items linked with travel onto the raffia or ribbon, and tie a simple cross-tie over the front of the gift package. Allow the objects to dangle on the front of the package.

ACCORDION-FOLD TISSUE WRAP

DESIGNER: MOLLY SIEBURG (BOX DESIGN BY PATRICE TAPPÉ)

*W*ith a few strategic folds, plain white tissue paper becomes a refined wrapping for simple boxes. Add a sheer organza ribbon and pressed pansies or a bouquet of lavender or ferns and simplicity turns spectacular.

Pressing Flowers

The pansies and ferns in this project can be pressed and left to dry in a flower press or a heavy phone book. Cut the flowers or ferns from their living plant while they are at peak condition. Place a sheet of wax paper at least two-thirds of the way through a phone book or other heavy book. Put the flowers on the paper, and arrange them with the most beautiful petals showing. Place another piece of wax paper on top of them and close the book carefully. Stack another book on top for weight, and leave the drying flowers for two weeks. The drying time will depend on the moisture in the air.

Pansy Wrap

INSTRUCTIONS

1. Measure the white tissue paper to fit your box, but don't cut the paper widthwise yet. Use at least two sheets to wrap each gift. Fold the paper accordion style in the middle, so that the folds will be positioned over the front. Leave every other fold a bit longer than the first.

2. Wrap and tape the box with the folds facing front.

3. Wrap a sheer ribbon around the length of the box, and attach it with tape on the back.

4. Place a spot of glue on the back of each pressed flower with your glue gun and press them down on the ribbon, spaced evenly apart.

Fern Wrap

INSTRUCTIONS

1. Wrap a box as usual with your accordion-folded tissue paper. You will need two different sizes of ribbon.

2. Wrap a piece of organza ribbon lengthwise, and attach it to the back of the box with tape.

3. Wrap one piece around the box widthwise, and tape it to the back of the box also.

4. Make a bow with the thinner of the two ribbons. Make four loops and leave two tails out of one long piece of ribbon.

5. Hold the bow together and tie it in place on the package with another piece of ribbon. Cut off the remaining ends until they are the same length as the first two tails. There will now be four.

6. Take several dried ferns and stick them in the bow where the ribbon is knotted together. Place a small amount of glue where they meet, so that the ferns will not slip out.

VARIATION

A lavender bundle tied into the bow of a matching organza ribbon creates a spectular tissue wrap. (See photo, far left.)

POSTAL WRAPS

Designer: Carol Stangler

These simple, yet carefully arranged packages call to mind the surprise of receiving a parcel in the mail. Save those old postcards and stamps from exotic places, which seem too precious to throw out. Choose from the same color scheme, or perhaps create a theme of all ocean scenes, mountain ranges, or cities-at-night scenes or create your own postcard collages.

YOU WILL NEED

- ❖ Brown paper bags
- ❖ Used postage stamps
- ❖ One to three used or new postcards
- ❖ Twine, string, or a colorful flat ribbon
- ❖ Cellophane tape
- ❖ Glue
- ❖ Scissors

Tips: If you use new postcards, tape them onto the box with double-sided cellophane tape, rather than gluing them. This way, the cards become part of the gift and can be removed for later use.

For a few dollars, you can pick up a collection of loose, canceled stamps through mail order or in specialty stores.

INSTRUCTIONS

1. Cut open a brown paper bag, and wrap your gift as usual.

2. Choose three postcards that go well together visually, and glue them onto the box so that they slightly overlap. You may angle them a bit for more effect.

3. Double or triple wrap twine or string around your package in two horizontal lines and two vertical lines, evenly spaced apart. Tie off the string into a knot, and clip the ends close to the knot.

4. Cut four pieces of twine, 4 inches (10 cm) long. Tie each of these at the four intersections where the vertical and horizontal strands of twine meet.

VARIATIONS

Glue used postage stamps onto your box instead. Try matching them to your gift recipient's personality—"famous men" stamps for your favorite man, nature stamps for the environmentalist, or commemorative stamps for the historian.

Use a postcard and color-coordinated stamp for your decoration. Glue them onto the package neatly, and tie a flat ribbon over the box across the postcard. The color of the ribbon should echo the predominant color of the package. Tie the ribbon into a knot, and cut the ends on a diagonal.

NATURAL BOOK COVER

DESIGNER: DANA HELDRETH

*S*omehow people always know that a gift-wrapped book is still a book, no matter how you try to hide it. Next time, don't disguise the fact, but make a dashing book cover instead. It's a beautiful way to display an unopened gift, and the cover will protect the book, even when the raffia ribbon and delicate dried flowers have been discarded.

INSTRUCTIONS

1. Choose a plain sheet of paper (you may vary your colors) thin enough to fold crisply at the edges. Place your book open on the paper and cut the paper, leaving 2 inches (5 cm) on each vertical side of the book, but allowing no extra paper on the horizontal edge. Fold the 2-inch (5 cm) strips over the inside of the front and back book cover, pinching the book cover and the paper together.

2. Cut two strips of decorative paper approximately 2 inches (5 cm) in width and the length of the open book, plus 2 inches (5 cm).

3. Measure 1 inch (2.5 cm) up from the bottom and 1 inch (2.5 cm) down from the top of the plain paper, and make a small mark with a pencil. Place the decorative paper over the plain paper at the marked points and fold the rest under, so that the decorative paper comes up 1 inch (2.5 cm) on the back side of the plain paper and crease. The decorative paper should run the length of the plain cover paper.

4. Spread glue on the plain paper under the 1-inch (2.5 cm) mark, and replace the decorative paper, burnishing or rubbing out any air bubbles or creases, with a scoring tool. (You may use the back of a spoon, or a bone folder used in bookmaking, which is available at craft or art stores.)

5. Fold the decorative paper over the back of the cover paper again, and glue. Once the decorative paper is smoothly affixed to the plain cover paper, fold both vertical edges over the book cover, and close the book. The cover will hold now. No glue or tape is necessary.

6. Using natural-colored raffia, wrap it around the book widthwise one or two times, depending on how thick you would like your "ribbon". Tie the raffia in a knot in front, leaving about 2 inches (5 cm) extra at each end to tie around the bow.

7. For the bow, cut 15 to 20 strands of raffia, 4 inches (10 cm) long. Bunch the strands together and tie them in the middle.

8. Place them onto the cover of the book, where you have tied the raffia ribbon into a knot. Using the 2-inch (5 cm) pieces of raffia on either end of the knot, tie the raffia bow onto the book cover.

9. Add your plant material last. (Tip: Use whatever you have available—perhaps sprigs of dried flowers, plants, and berries.) Arrange them in a fan shape, pointing towards the top of the book. Place a dot of glue on the bottom part of the stems, and tuck them under the raffia bow.

Tips: If you use handmade paper, be sure to choose one which is flexible enough to fold over the book cover easily.

Try a complementary color of raffia to go with your paper.

Invert the papers, using a more decorative paper as your main cover paper, and a lighter, plainer paper for the edges.

Use fabric instead of paper, for a more durable and alternative cover.

ROSETTE PIN AND WALLPAPER

DESIGNER: MYRNA HARRIGAN

*T*his wallpaper wrapping creates a sleek and unrumpled texture on a plain box. Remove the rosette, and you have a brooch to wear on your lapel.

YOU WILL NEED

- ❖ 1 sheet of smooth-textured wallpaper or commercial wrapping paper
- ❖ 1 yard (.9 m) pink wired ribbon, 1½ inches (3.8 cm) wide
- ❖ ⅓ yard (30 cm) green wired ribbon, 1½ inches (3.8 cm) wide
- ❖ Matching or complementary ribbon, long enough to wrap around your gift box
- ❖ 1 pin (found in craft stores)
- ❖ Thread
- ❖ Needle
- ❖ Glue gun and glue sticks
- ❖ Scissors

INSTRUCTIONS

1. Wrap your gift box as usual. Wrap the ribbon without wires around the box, and either glue one end over the top of the other with the hot glue gun, or sew the ends together with needle and thread. This way the band will slide off the box and can be slipped back on later.

2. Using 1 yard (.9 m) of pink wired ribbon and a needle and thread, run a basting stitch along one edge of the ribbon as close to the wire as possible.

3. Pull the thread tightly to gather the ribbon. Starting in the center, make a spiral which forms a rise in the center. Baste it to hold the center in place.

4. Using 6 inches (15 cm) of green ribbon for each leaf, fold each strip of ribbon in half to mark the center.

5. Fold each half forward, forming a point at the top and making a diagonal line on each side.

6. Turn the ribbon over and, using a thin piece of wire, tie it about 1 inch (2.5 cm) from the tip. Attach this to the back of the flower with a needle and thread.

7. Repeat these steps with one or two more leaves. Add a piece of ribbon at the back of the bow to cover the stitching, and sew a pin to the back of the ribbon. (You can use the hot glue for this instead, if you wish.)

8. Pin the ribbon onto the band on top of the box. The band, along with the fabric rose, can be slipped off the gift box without being taken apart.

DUAL-COLOR ROUND WRAP

DESIGNER: NICOLE TUGGLE

Ever been faced with wrapping a circular container? It's not as daunting as it seems. With gorgeous flexible paper that gathers around the box in soft pleats, this wrapping is both elegant and functional. So don't just dump those boxes of truffles or tins of cookies and petit fours into a bag—swaddle them lovingly in handmade paper, and make this gift memorable.

YOU WILL NEED

❖ 2 large sheets of handmade paper in complementary or contrasting colors

❖ Organza ribbon

❖ Scissors

❖ Cellophane tape

Tips: Create gentle, soft pleats by leaving a bit of slack in the paper while gathering, and space them farther apart.

For pleats with a busier, more-tailored appearance, crease the sides of the pleats with your fingers as you gather, and make more pleats with smaller spaces in between.

INSTRUCTIONS

1. Fold the two sheets of flexible paper in half along the diagonal, and place them side by side with a 1¼-inch (3.2 cm) overlap. Tape them in place.

2. Center your container on the overlap, and fold the paper in half.

3. Gather the left-hand sheet toward the center in evenly spaced pleats. (**Tip:** You may wish to vary the size and spacing of the gathers depending on the size of your box and the look you wish to achieve. For the simplest wrapping, create larger gathers.)

4. Do the same with the opposite side, and twist both sheets together where they meet at the top.

5. Cut approximately 12 inches (30 cm) of organza ribbon, and tie a simple bow around the gathered ends, on the side of the package with the pleats.

VARIATION

Try a stiffer paper for a crisper looking package. Be sure to crease the pleats with even spacing between each one. Match a crisper ribbon with this paper, or try using multiple strands of curly ribbon in place of a bow.

ASIAN DUAL BOTTLE WRAP

DESIGNER: MAGGIE ROTMAN

An ingenious way to wrap two bottles, this Asian fabric wrapping is both appealing and practical. Use a large dish towel, and make it part of the gift.

YOU WILL NEED
❖ One large piece of printed fabric

INSTRUCTIONS

1. Place two bottles together on the diagonal of your fabric. Wrap the cloth around the bottles.

2. Stand the bottles up, and twist the cloth above the bottles.

3. Cross the ends of the cloth over the side with the loose flap, and wrap the ends around the middle of the bottles.

4. Turn the bottles around and tie the ends at the back.

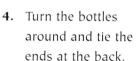

GARDENING CATALOG GIFTWRAP

DESIGNER: CAROL STANGLER

F or that special gardener in your life, or your best green-thumbed friend, this wrapping is convenient, economical, and a personal tribute to your good friend's favorite hobby. Feel free to expand on this theme by using the pages of other catalogs.

INSTRUCTIONS

1. Cut open a brown paper bag that is large enough to enclose your package. Wrap and tape your box.

2. Open a garden catalog to the middle pages and pull out the center staples so that you have one long sheet (usually 11 x 17 inches (28 x 43.5 cm) if the catalog is standard size.) Choose pages which are especially colorful or relate to the gift recipient's gardening interests.

> YOU WILL NEED
> ❖ Brown paper bags
> ❖ Pages from a gardening catalog
> ❖ Green gardening twine
> ❖ Tape
> ❖ Craft Glue
> ❖ Scissors

3. Spread a thin line of glue around the edges of the catalog page, and paste it diagonally onto the wrapped box.

4. Cut out images of large flowers and paste them onto the package.

5. Double or triple tie the package with green twine. Arrange the ends of the twine, and glue them onto the package in an attractive position.

FISH AND SALAMANDER PICTURE BOXES

DESIGNER: DANA HELDRETH

Collages made of cutout images from magazines, decorative paper, twigs, and dried foliage look fresh and modern. These boxes wouldn't look out of place on a shelf or mantel in someone's home. Because the decoration appears only on the box lid, it won't be disturbed when the gift is opened, enabling the gift recipient to keep the box for further use.

Framed Fish Boxes

INSTRUCTIONS

1. Paint your chosen boxes with the black spray paint or poster paint. Allow good ventilation for spray painting, and be sure to spread out newspaper to catch the splatters. Paint the outside of the boxes completely, including the edges, and allow them to dry overnight.

> **YOU WILL NEED**
> ❖ Cardboard boxes of varying sizes
> ❖ Can of black spray paint, or poster paint
> ❖ Newspapers
> ❖ Magazines
> ❖ Scrap paper
> ❖ Dried plant material (twigs, straw, leaves, petals)
> ❖ Craft glue
> ❖ Glue brush
> ❖ Scissors
> ❖ Burnishing tool (optional)

2. For the smaller fish-themed boxes, measure the top of your box lid, leaving a 1-inch (2.5 cm) border for the frame you will later add. Leaf through a magazine, and cut out images which appeal to you. You may decide upon a wildlife theme, flowers, or other subjects.

3. Cut out strips of designs in colors complementary to your main subject. They should measure approximately ½ inch (1.3 cm) in width and should be the exact length of the sides of your image or the box itself. These will compose the "frame."

4. Lightly brush glue along the edges of your main image, and center the square of paper on the box lid. Put a sheet of scrap paper over the image and smooth over it with your fingers or a burnishing tool. This way fingerprints won't ruin the glossy magazine paper.

5. Frame the central image with the strips of border paper. Remove and lightly brush the back sides with glue. Place them back around the image, and smooth these strips with the scrap paper. (Note: You may wish to leave an intentional space around the central image as a variation. Be sure to measure all sides evenly before gluing.)

6. Add your plant material last. Sparingly, add glue to twigs and place them around the central image, towards the edges of the box. They will create another frame.

Salamander Silhouette Box

INSTRUCTIONS

1. Cut silhouettes of images out of a magazine and set aside.

2. Place the lid of your box onto a sheet of decorative paper and measure, leaving 2 inches (5 cm) beyond the actual lid edges, and mark. (Note: Depending on the depth of the lid, you may need to leave more or less paper in order to fold under the edges of the lid.)

> ADDITIONAL SUPPLIES
> ❖ One sheet of decorative paper

3. Wrap the paper around the lid as you would wrap a basic gift, folding the sides in and the top flap over and under the box lid to make sure it fits. To avoid wrinkling, brush glue just along the edges of your paper and rewrap, making sure the paper fits smoothly along the inside edges of the lid.

4. Spray paint the bottom and sides of the box which will be showing, and allow it to dry. Try different arrangements of the images on top of the box before you glue.

5. Once everything is glued down, place scrap paper over the collage and smooth over it.

6. Arrange decorative twigs on the box, and glue them down.

Gift Traditions from Around the World

Southern Syrian Christmas Tradition (Epiphany Eve, January 5)
On the evening of January 5, children are told that the camel of Jesus—apparently the youngest of those that carried the Three Wise Men to the manger in Bethlehem—travels over the desert bringing gifts. The children are instructed to leave bowls of water and wheat by their doorways. Upon awakening, good children find the water and wheat gone, and gifts in their stead. Bad children find a mark on their wrist.

Hong Kong, Moon Day (the 15th day of the 8th moon of the year, August–September)
A traditional gift exchanged between friends and acquaintances on Moon Day are sweet desserts called "moon cakes." These cakes are composed of fruit and other sweets, wrapped in a thin crust in the shape of a full moon, about 2 or 3 inches (5 or 7.5 cm) in diameter and ½ inch (1.3 cm) thick.

In ancient times, when a Confucian scholar was hired to teach in the family school, the teacher presented moon cakes to each of his students. The families gave him a red envelope filled with money in return.

Romanian Day of the Dead (May 31)
Alms are given away to guarantee the serenity of dead souls. These gifts, or *dari*, often include small coins, earthenware containers, pitchers, and dishes adorned with flowers and herbs, and filled with food and wine. Dari are customarily given easily to friends and acquaintances. One can also give a gift for one's own soul.

SPRAY PAINTED FERNS

DESIGNER: SUSAN KINNEY

A luminescent background gives way to whispery silhouettes of ferns and forest matter with this quick "wrapping" technique. The stylish containers you create can be used long after the gift within is removed.

INSTRUCTIONS

1. Spread out newsprint in a well-ventilated area, and cover the exterior of your container with the black spray paint. Let the container dry for several hours.

YOU WILL NEED

❖ Plain cardboard or metal boxes and containers
❖ Can of black spray paint
❖ Can of gold or copper metallic spray paint
❖ Branches of ferns and other leafy plants
❖ Newsprint

2. Place a leafy branch onto one side of the container and spray the metallic paint over the branch and side of the box. Allow this to dry.

3. Turn the container to another side, and use a leafy branch to create another silhouette design. Allow it to dry, and repeat this pattern on all sides.

TWISTED-KNOT FABRIC WRAP

DESIGNER: MAGGIE ROTMAN

*F*lexible paper or fabric lends itself well to this fun and functional vestment for square boxes or odd-shaped objects. With only a few twists and a quick knot, your wrapping is done.

YOU WILL NEED

- ❖ Tissue paper
- ❖ Square of thin fabric or flexible handmade paper
- ❖ Strip of complementary or contrasting fabric
- ❖ Rubber band
- ❖ Tape
- ❖ Scissors

Tips: Try this wrapping on oddly shaped objects. If the object is too awkward for tissue paper wrapping, then forgo it and use only the fabric wrapping.

INSTRUCTIONS

1. Wrap your boxed gift in colored tissue paper. The milky paper or fabric will allow the color to show through the fully wrapped package.

2. Place the tissue-wrapped box in the middle of your fabric or handmade paper. Be sure that your fabric extends about 6 inches (15 cm) beyond the center of the box top.

3. Gather up all the fabric around the box until you have a bunch of fabric in the top center of the box. Pay attention to the folds on the sides of the box, and arrange them attractively.

4. Twist the bunch of fabric several times, then wrap the end around the twist. Tuck the ends under a rubber band. The knot on top should be symmetrical.

5. Wrap a strip of cloth around the topknot once or twice, and tuck the remaining end under the wrapped strip.

The wise man does not lay up treasure.
The more he gives, the more he has. –Chinese Proverb

PARTY POPPER TUBE WRAP

DESIGNER: LISA SANDERS

*M*ake these festive tubes to house lightweight gifts. They are also ideal for holding letters, handmade coupons, and invitations. Imagine a table with a small party popper favor at each place setting. Your guests may never be so delighted again.

YOU WILL NEED

- ❖ Commercial wrapping paper
- ❖ Cardboard tube
- ❖ Tissue paper
- ❖ Curling ribbon
- ❖ Tape
- ❖ Scissors

INSTRUCTIONS

1. Wrap your gift in giftwrap or tissue paper, and insert it into the tube. Crumple some tissue paper and stuff it into the tube at each end to keep the gift from falling out.

2. Cut six squares of tissue paper, approximately 12 inches square (30 cm square) for a large tube, and smaller for a smaller-sized tube. Fold the tissue paper into quarters, and twist the end where the folds meet.

3. Tape the twisted ends of the tissue paper inside the ends of the tube. Use three pieces for each end of the tube.

4. Cut the curling ribbon into 18 lengths, about 6 inches (15 cm) longer than the tube. Use several different colors for the best effect.

5. Tape the curling ribbon along the length of the tube, letting the ribbon extend beyond the ends of the tube, about 3 inches (7.6 cm) at each end. Spread the rows of ribbon out so that they are evenly spaced around the tube. Curl the ends of some of the ribbons.

6. Cut a piece of wrapping paper about 6 inches (15 cm) longer than the tube and wide enough to wrap around the tube with an overlap. Fold one cut edge under ½ inch (1.3 cm) to make a neat edge.

7. Cut a 3-inch-deep (7.6 cm) fringe in each end of the paper.

8. Wrap the paper around the tube, ending with the edge which has been folded under. Tape it in place.

COLLAGE WRAP

DESIGNER: BARBARA BUSSOLARI

*M*ake the card the focal point of this giftwrap. This stacked collage made of natural materials is unique enough to be detached and saved. It can even be framed as a piece of art. Affix a pin to the back, and a new gift appears in the form of a brooch.

INSTRUCTIONS

1. Wrap your package as usual with a sheet of handmade paper or commercial wrapping paper. Crease each seam to make sharp folds.

2. Cut a piece of card stock for your gift card that best fits the size of your box. Keep in mind the size of your package and the background. If you choose a dark color for the outside of your card, choose a lighter color for the interior. Cut it slightly smaller than the exterior, and glue it inside for your message.

3. Cover the top of your card with handmade, hand-decorated, or commercial paper. Give the card dimension by cutting pieces of mat board with a craft knife. Vary the sizes so that the board can be stacked in ascending order. Run a dark permanent marker along the cut edges to cover the naked board. Cover the boards with decorative paper.

YOU WILL NEED

- ❖ Handmade paper, or commercial wrapping paper
- ❖ Card stock
- ❖ Mat board
- ❖ Acrylic gloss medium
- ❖ Buttons
- ❖ Beads
- ❖ Natural materials, such as wood, lichen, shells
- ❖ Raffia
- ❖ Craft glue or glue stick
- ❖ Permanent marker
- ❖ Glue gun and glue sticks
- ❖ Tape
- ❖ Paintbrush
- ❖ Craft knife
- ❖ Scissors

4. Brush acrylic medium onto the top of the card and the mat board pieces. Two coats will work best. After the coating dries, glue the mat board pieces onto one another, and add beads and your natural materials to the top. Glue them down with the glue gun.

5. Glue the card on the top of your wrapped gift box.

6. Tie a raffia bow around the box.

Making a Small Gift Bag

INSTRUCTIONS

1. Measure your paper against the cassette cases. Cut one end of the paper with the deckle-edged scissors to make a decorated top of the bag.

2. Tape two cassette cases together as the base for the small bag. Line up the top of the paper with the top of the cassette cases. Leave enough of an overlap on the bottom to fold the paper, as you would in wrapping a package.

3. Wrap the paper around the cases to form a tube, and tape it in the back. (Double-sided tape will work best in this instance.)

4. Fold the ends down and tape them. Slip the bag off of the cassette cases, and crease the sides so that they bend

YOU WILL NEED
* Sturdy handmade or commercial wrapping paper
* Raffia
* 2 cassette cases
* Tape
* Craft glue
* Deckle-edged scissors
* Scissors
* Hole punch or awl

inward. (Use a regular paper grocery bag as an example.)

5. Punch holes in the top of the bag, and thread raffia through it. Tie the raffia into a bow, in either the front or the back.

6. Create the collage as in the first set of instructions, and glue a pin to the back. Pin it to the front of the bag.

FABRIC ENVELOPE

DESIGNER: MAGGIE ROTMAN

*O*ne of the most refined types of Japanese wrappings, this technique uses no knots, glue, tape, or other means to hold the fabric together. Best used on flat objects, this wrapping is lauded for its clean lines and simplicity.

YOU WILL NEED
❖ Square piece of fabric, three times the size of your gift
❖ Buttons
❖ Craft glue

INSTRUCTIONS

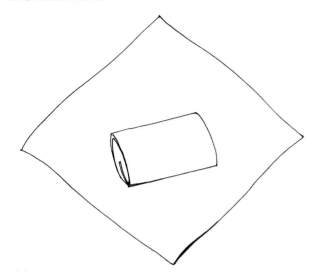

1. Center the gift in the lower corner of the fabric.

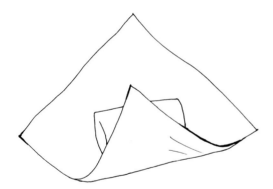

2. Place the lower corner over the gift.

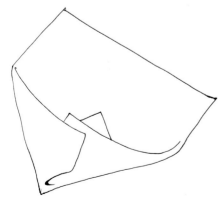

3. Place the left corner over the gift.

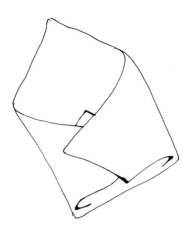

4. Place the right corner over the gift.

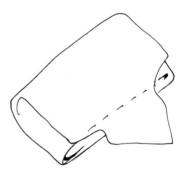

5. Bring the upper corner flap down over the gift, and tuck the excess cloth into the fold.

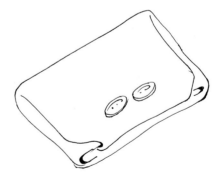

6. Glue on two decorative buttons.

VARIATION

To achieve the look of our project photo, fold the corner flaps in towards the center at a 45° angle.

LACE-COVERED GIFT BOX

DESIGNER: LISA SANDERS

A delicate lace gift box made to last, is a special gift indeed. Fill it with silk slips or something naughtier for the bride-to-be. Bedazzle any lady with this handmade container.

YOU WILL NEED

❖ Pasteboard box
❖ Can of spray paint, gold
❖ Acrylic paint, white
❖ Assorted lace
❖ Narrow decorative braid
❖ Craft glue
❖ Clear acrylic polyurethane
❖ Scissors
❖ 1½-inch wide (3.8 cm) paintbrush

INSTRUCTIONS

1. Spray paint the inside of the box and lid with the gold paint.

2. Paint the outside of the box with the white acrylic paint, using two coats.

3. Draw or score a faint line where the edge of the lid meets the box.

4. Cut out lace motifs and glue them to the box. Trim away the excess lace at the edges of the lid and along the line where the lid edge meets the box.

5. Glue the decorative braid along the edge of the lid and bottom of the box.

6. Let the glue dry thoroughly.

7. Separate the lid from the box, and paint the box and lid with clear polyurethane (to protect the lace and make it easy to clean).

Tip: You can dye the lace in strong tea. Depending on how strong the tea is and how long it is left in the tea, your lace will range in color from light to dark beige.

WHITE ON WHITE PEARLS AND TULLE

DESIGNER: BRINDA CALDWELL

*N*ever underestimate the power of white. Layers of white in pearls, tulle, smooth paper, and corded ribbon recall a wedding, bridal shower, anniversary gift, or any elegant occasion.

YOU WILL NEED

❖ 1 sheet of printed commercial wrapping paper, white
❖ White tulle with gold flecks
❖ Wired "pearls"
❖ White and gold tassel
❖ Glue gun and glue sticks
❖ Tape
❖ Scissors

INSTRUCTIONS

1. Wrap your gift with the commercial paper. Make sure the print of the paper is going the proper direction on the box.

2. Cut a piece of tulle long enough to tie into a simple bow.

3. Tie another piece of tulle around the first bow, and tie the tulle into another bow perpendicular to the first.

4. Make four loops with the flexible wired pearls, and place them onto the bows. Tie another piece of tulle into a bow around the first two bows and the pearls.

5. Cut several strands of the wired pearls, and glue them to the base of the tulle with your glue gun.

6. Glue or tie the cord and tassel onto the package.

PASTEL PAPER KNOTS

DESIGNER NICOLE TUGGLE

Soft and pliable unryu paper, in spring-like pastels, makes this wrapping so exceptional. You can use any type of flexible handmade paper to achieve similar effects, as long as it can be tied into a knot without tearing.

YOU WILL NEED

- Unryu paper, or other pliable hand-made paper, in white, lavender, and green
- Tape
- Scissors

INSTRUCTIONS

1. Wrap your box as you usual, using any one of the colors as your base.

2. Take a sheet of a contrasting color and cut it slightly narrower than the width of the box. Make sure it reaches all the way around the box.

3. Wrap the strip of paper around the box and tape it in the back.

4. Cut a narrower strip of paper, the same color as the first wrapping, approximately 6 inches (15 cm) wide, and long enough to wrap around the width of the box.

5. Wrap the box from front to back with the strip in the center of the box, and tape the overlapping ends together in back.

6. Cut a small strip of paper measuring 2 x 6 inches (5 x 15 cm), matching it to the second sheet of paper you used. Tie the narrow strip around the middle of the paper strip you have just wrapped around the box. Pull the knot tight, so that the paper will be narrower in the middle. Tuck the tied ends into the knot itself.

VARIATION

Tie several strips of paper into knots along the piece of paper wrapped around the center of the box. Try alternating colors or making knots of all different colors.

Gifts should be handed, not hurled. —Danish Proverb

CORRUGATED CARDBOARD TUBULAR GIFT BOX

DESIGNER: NICOLE TUGGLE

*H*ere's a simple gift box for you to construct. Made of corrugated cardboard, it is ideal for the small gift item, and the boxes can be used again and again. These appealing containers can be decorated with raffia, twine, ribbon, or a whimsical dangling bauble.

INSTRUCTIONS

1. Using the template on page 126, enlarge or reduce the pattern on a copier to the desired size. Keep in mind that the paper stock or cardboard needs to be thick enough to hold its shape, yet flexible enough to bend smoothly.

2. Trace the package shape and all lines onto tracing paper. Place on the wrong side of the cardboard, and cut out the package shape.

3. With the tracing paper in place, cut out the container shape, and mark the curved fold lines by pricking small holes through the cardboard with the point of your craft knife.

4. Score along the pricked, curved line. Then score a line through the center of the package. Crease inwards along the center of the scored line.

5. Fold the long edge inward on the markings and apply glue to the flap. Bring the opposite long edge over the flap. Place a weight, such as a book, on top, and allow the glue to dry for one hour. (Note: A glue stick is fast and simple, but generally won't hold as long as craft glue.)

6. Gently squeeze the sides of the package, forcing the box to open slightly. At one end, fold in the curved flaps along the scored lines. Press them into place, with one resting on top of the other. Insert your gift, and close the other end in the same manner.

7. Tie raffia, twine, or thin ribbon around the completed package. Make sure that the twine is wrapped snugly around the ends so that the flaps do not open.

VARIATIONS

Use the same template, but extend the length of the package to achieve a different shape—ideal for gifts, such as pens, tapers, incense, and more.

Cut out various shapes, such as hearts, stars, or moons, in contrasting colors of paper or cardboard, and glue them to the outside of the packages.

Embellish the packages with stones, beads, buttons, acorns, pinecones, an old piece of junk jewelry, or anything that can be tied to the ribbon or glued to the front.

MESH POT

DESIGNER: TRACI NEIL-TAYLOR

So simple and yet so grand—a bit of mesh material and a flowerpot is all it takes to transform an ordinary gift into an extraordinary one. The mesh is reminiscent of a flashy garden hat.

YOU WILL NEED

❖ Piece of mesh material
❖ Flowerpot
❖ Potpourri
❖ Cinnamon stick
❖ Raffia
❖ Scissors

Tip: Wrap your gift in tissue paper before placing it in the pot. The more wrapping, the more suspense.

INSTRUCTIONS

1. Place your flowerpot onto the mesh fabric. Measure a square of mesh, large enough to wrap the flowerpot with a little extra material for the flourish. [For an average-sized flowerpot, measure 24 inches square (62 cm square).]

2. Place the flowerpot with your gift inside into the center of the mesh square. Sprinkle potpourri over the gift to conceal the contents.

3. Bring the four corners of the square of mesh together in the middle, close to the mouth of the pot.

4. Gather the mesh together, forming a "neck," and tie several pieces of raffia around it in a knot.

5. Push the cinnamon stick through the raffia tie.

6. Arrange the stiff mesh so that it stands high and wide for extra pizzazz.

VARIATIONS

Link your surface decoration with something in the gift. Does your gift have something to do with cooking? Stick a wooden cooking spoon through the raffia knot. For a friend with a sweet tooth, embellish the tie with a lollipop or licorice stick.

TUSSIE MUSSIE

DESIGNER: BRINDA CALDWELL

*A*s sweetly old-fashioned as its name, this delicate Victorian bouquet tops a hand-
painted box. The container stands on its own and can be given as the actual
gift with a few sachets inside.

INSTRUCTIONS

1. Spread out newsprint in a well-ventilated area, and spray paint the exterior of the plain box and lid. Let it dry completely.

2. Place your gift inside the box, and tie the wire ribbon around the box on a diagonal. Glue the knot to the top of the box.

3. Glue the tussie mussie to the top of the box.

4. Make four or five small loops in the ribbon, tying them together with a smaller piece of ribbon at the base of the loops. Glue them to the top of the box, between the flowers and stems of the tussie mussie.

YOU WILL NEED

❖ Small octagonal-shaped box
❖ Can of mahogany spray paint
❖ Translucent wire ribbon
❖ Silk flower store-bought tussie-mussie
❖ Newsprint
❖ Glue gun and glue sticks
❖ Scissors

VARIATIONS

You can create your own tussie mussie, using silk flowers. Bundle them together and cut the stems to a desired length to fit the box. Tie the flowers into a bundle at the base of the pods with a small unobtrusive ribbon or wire.

BEADED CURLY RIBBONS

DESIGNER: MYRNA HARRIGAN

*I*f this doesn't say "party," then nothing does! A winning combination of splashy wrapping paper, cascades of multi-colored ribbons, and cheerful beads, ensures that this gift will be the life of the party.

INSTRUCTIONS

1. Wrap your gift as usual. Match several different colors of curly ribbon to the paper you have used, and cut them long enough to fit around the package. Leave a good bit of excess to curl later.

> **YOU WILL NEED**
> ❖ Festive wrapping paper
> ❖ Curly ribbon, various colors
> ❖ Beads, various colors
> ❖ Scissors

2. Match up eight or ten strands of ribbon, and wrap them around the sides of the package. Tie off the ends on top, and leave about 6 inches (15 cm) on each side. Tie an equal amount of strands around the other two sides of the box, and tie the ends together at the top, intersecting the other tied ribbon.

3. String a colorful bead onto two strands of ribbon near the ends, and tie them so that the bead will not slip off. Continue stringing beads onto the rest of the ribbons.

4. Cut 20 strands of curly ribbon 30 inches (76 cm) long. Tie the strands around the knot of ribbon on top of the package.

5. Using the blade of your scissors, curl the ribbon from its base where it is knotted to the tips. Repeat to achieve a tight curl.

VARIATIONS

Tie other trinkets onto the ends of the ribbon, such as buttons, exotic coins (with a hole in the middle, as some Asian coins have), and other dangles.

CYLINDRICAL PAPER BOW LACE-UP

DESIGNER: VADIM BORA

*W*rap *a tin of cookies or any cylindrical package for a look that ranges from fancy country style to marvelously modern. The ties which lace up the decorative cardboard are actually unfurled twisted paper ribbon.*

YOU WILL NEED

❖ Commercial wrapping paper
❖ Twisted paper ribbon
❖ Corrugated cardboard
❖ Tape
❖ Ruler
❖ Pencil
❖ Scissors
❖ Hole punch

Tip: If your gift is not perfectly symmetrical, use some corrugated cardboard to surround the object. Tape it together, so that it creates a vertical frame around the item, then wrap it as in Step 1, and continue with the instructions.

INSTRUCTIONS

1. Place your gift on the commercial wrapping paper, and roll the paper around the cylindrical object. Cut the paper so that the edges meet in back, and so that there is at least an excess of 6 inches (15 cm) on either end.

2. Tape the wide ends of the paper together around the object. Fold the bottom paper inward, and tape it down.

3. Gather the excess paper on top, and tie a piece of unfurled twisted paper ribbon around the base. Tie it off and make a bow, looping only one side and partially pulling it through.

4. Cut the corrugated cardboard to fit from edge to edge, from top to bottom, of the container. Measure it around the container so that there is a ½-inch (1.3 cm) space between the sides of the cardboard.

5. Measure the vertical edge of the paper with a ruler, and make marks 2 inches (5 cm) apart. Cut triangles into the edge, with the tips at each 2-inch (5 cm) mark. Repeat these cuts on the other side, making sure they align perfectly with the opposite side.

6. Punch holes in the tips of the triangles, and wrap the cardboard around the cylinder.

7. Thread a 6-inch (15 cm) twisted paper ribbon through holes opposing each other. Unfurl the twisted paper and tie each piece together.

ROUND AND SQUARE FABRIC WRAPS

DESIGNER: PEI-LING BECKER

*P*lagued with wrapping a round object? Use this ancient Asian fabric wrapping method, which was once used to carry heavy watermelons to and from the market. Fashion a square wrap, using a similar method.

Round Wrap

YOU WILL NEED

❖ Square or rectangular piece of fabric

Tips: Pull the knots together snugly, so that they won't slip apart. Be sure to fluff the ends. You can also spray starch on them to keep them stiff.

VARIATION

Make a fan (signifying prosperity in Asian tradition) out of stiff paper, by alternating the sides you fold vertically. Attach it to the top of wrap.

INSTRUCTIONS

1. Place the round gift you are wrapping in the center of the cloth, and bring the two corners of the cloth together on either side of the object.

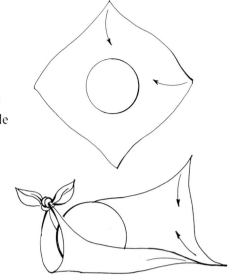

2. Tie the corners on one side of the cloth together, knotting the ends evenly. Repeat on the other side with the remaining two corners.

3. Pass the first knot under the second and pull the cloth tight around the ball, forming a sling. (See illustrations at right.)

Square Wrap

YOU WILL NEED

❖ Square or rectangular piece of fabric
❖ Thick cord

INSTRUCTIONS

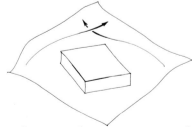

1. Place your box on a square of fabric and pull the left and right corners of the fabric over the box.

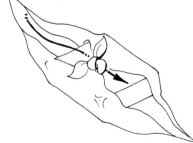

2. Tie the corners into a knot, and pull the top corner under the knot.

3. Tie the bottom corner of the fabric to the top corner and tuck underneath the first knot. Wrap a piece of cord around the knot.

WOVEN PACKAGE WRAP AND GIFT TAG

DESIGNER: BARBARA BUSSOLARI

*H*ere's a unique wrapping that will allow you to use your collection of natural materials. This particular sample was entirely hand-woven, but it's easy to achieve a similar look by using a loosely woven fabric into which you can "weave" bits of thread, plant material, Spanish moss, strips of rag, straw, twigs, and more.

YOU WILL NEED

- ❖ Hand-woven piece of material (a loosely woven place mat can be used as a substitute)
- ❖ Strips of rags
- ❖ Raffia
- ❖ Twigs
- ❖ Thread
- ❖ Beads
- ❖ Buttons
- ❖ Straw or Spanish moss
- ❖ Thin-gauge wire
- ❖ Card stock, black
- ❖ Text-weight paper
- ❖ Tapestry needle
- ❖ Awl
- ❖ Glue gun and glue sticks
- ❖ Scissors

INSTRUCTIONS

1. Thread a tapestry needle with raffia, thread, or strips of rag that will fit through the eye of the needle. Use a running stitch to weave the items of your choice through the material. Weave twigs in and out of the material, from one end to the other.

2. Wrap the material around the gift box. Sew the two ends of the material together with a simple stitch at the back of the box.

3. Stitch the sides closed. A quick snip with some scissors will allow you to open the gift.

4. Make a bow out of strips of rags by cutting them uniformly, about 6 inches (15 cm) long and 1 inch (2.5 cm) wide. Put the strips together, and wrap a thread or wire around the middle of the bunch. Thread it through the top corner of your giftwrap, so that it holds snugly, or use hot glue.

5. Thread three beads onto a thin wire, 10 inches (25 cm) long. Insert it into a flat bone bead or button. Glue the beads down so that they remain in place. Twist the extra wire around a thick needle and release it for a curly accent. Glue the button to a small bunch of straw or Spanish moss, and glue the "nest" into the center of the bow.

6. Cut your card stock 3 inches (7.5 cm) long, and fold it in half in the middle. Cut the text-weight paper, slightly smaller than the black card stock. Glue the paper to the card stock, and fold both in half, with the text paper inside.

7. Glue three small beads or buttons down the front of the tag. Place a small dot of glue on the bottom tip of the tag, and insert it under the edge of the bow.

A generous action is its own reward. –English Proverb

STAR LACE-UP WALLPAPER WRAP

DESIGNER: VADIM BORA

*S*turdy wallpaper, cut into a star pattern and laced up with cord or ribbon, shows free design at its best. Black corrugated cardboard contrasts with the rosy paper, and vertical lines play in striking harmony with the satin illusion of the wallpaper.

INSTRUCTIONS

1. Measure the corrugated cardboard to fit the front of your gift box. Tape it to the box.

2. Measure the wallpaper to fit your box by wrapping it around the box until the ends touch. Mark the place on the paper where it folds over the sides of the box by creasing it vertically with your fingers.

3. Cut the paper at each corner, at a right angle to the long side. Divide the edge into four evenly spaced quadrants, and cut the paper to the edge of the box at each quadrant, as in figure 1.

4. Cut and fold the paper using figure 1 as your guide.

Figure 1

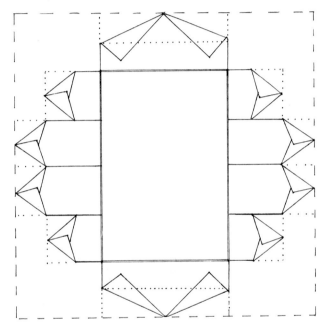

Figure 2

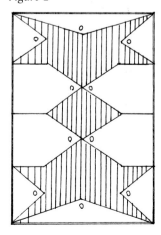

5. Punch holes in the tips of the triangles, and fold them all towards the center of the box.

6. Lace the cord or ribbon through opposing triangles and tie.

VARIATIONS

Look through your wallpaper scraps and choose any color combination you like. Match or contrast your corrugated cardboard.

QUICK KNEE-HIGH WRAPS

DESIGNER: SUSAN KINNEY

*Y*ou almost forgot about the party, and now there's no time now to stop at the store for wrapping paper! Quick, rummage through your drawers and haul out those colorful knee-highs or stockings that you never wear. With a few pulls and tucks and twists, a bottle of wine or candle turns into the perfect translucently-wrapped house gift.

YOU WILL NEED
- ❖ Colored knee-high stockings
- ❖ Raffia

INSTRUCTIONS

1. Choose two bright and complementary colors of stockings.

2. Pull the darker stocking over your gift, such as a wine or bath oil bottle, or candle, from the bottom up.

3. For a bottle, pull the top of the knee-high over the top of the bottle and gather the elastic end together at the neck. Tie a piece of raffia around the gathered end of the stocking. Fold the ribbed top of the stocking back once and fluff it into a "flower".

4. Wrap a pillar candle by pulling the stocking over the candle from the bottom up. Tie the top into a knot and fluff the remaining nylon fabric. Tie another stocking in contrasting color around the top third of the candle. Tie the stocking into a bow, or create another "flower" by folding the ribbed top of the stocking back once.

VELLUM ENVELOPE WRAP

Designer: Nicole Tuggle

A gift tag can play a large role in wrapping; this one is powerful enough to use as the sole decorative element of a plainly wrapped box. We've added fun trinkets to the mix of geometric patterns.

INSTRUCTIONS

1. Choose a template from page 126 and enlarge it on a photocopier to the desired size. Cut out the template.

YOU WILL NEED

- ❖ Text-weight paper
- ❖ Wrapping paper, handmade or commercial
- ❖ Vellum in purple, pewter, and green (available in art-supply stores)
- ❖ Craft glue or glue stick
- ❖ Ruler
- ❖ Tape
- ❖ Scissors

2. Place the template on the decorative vellum and trace the outline.

3. Cut the pattern out of the vellum. Fold and crease the sides as indicated on the template.

4. Fold in the two sides first. Then glue the bottom flap to the sides with craft glue or a glue stick.

5. Cut a piece of text-weight paper to fit inside the envelope, and write your note on it. Arrange the envelope on the box and tape it down.

VARIATIONS

Stack several pieces of vellum in varying colors on top of your gift box. The envelope should be the last to be taped on. Glue a flat trinket to the top for extra flair.

Punch a hole in one corner of a vellum envelope and thread a ribbon through the hole. Then tie the envelope around the package with the ribbon.

MAGNUM BOTTLE WRAP

DESIGNER: VADIM BORA

A magnum of champagne may speak for itself, but it still doesn't have the wow-factor of this fabulous natural wrap. Any oversized bottle will do, and it's a surefire guarantee that the contents won't be opened and imbibed right away.

INSTRUCTIONS

1. Place your gift bottle onto a sheet of two-sided handmade paper to measure the height and width you will need to cut. Make sure you actually role the paper around the bottle, leaving some overlap, so that you can get the proper measurement.

YOU WILL NEED

- ❖ Reversible hand-made paper (available at art-supply stores)
- ❖ Natural place mat
- ❖ Twine
- ❖ Toilet paper tube, optional
- ❖ Tape
- ❖ Scissors

2. Cut the paper and leave an excess of 6 inches (15 cm) at the top of the bottle.

3. Wrap the bottle with the paper. Gather the paper and the bottom and tape it flat, so that the bottle can sit up.

4. Before you tape the paper around the bottle, place a card-board tube (such as a toilet paper roll) over the neck of the bottle, which will give the neck a thicker frame.

5. Take a piece of twine and wrap it around the new "neck" of the bottle from the top to the bottom. You may choose to use several pieces of twine. Tie the knots in the front for a more interesting texture.

6. Wrap a place mat around the bottle. Thread a piece of twine through the place mat (or around it, if it is not loosely woven) around the bottom third of the bottle. Tie it into place.

7. Fold back the top corner of the place mat and the corner down with twine. Tie the twine into a bow.

8. Turn the handmade paper back at the top so that it looks like a collar or an ornate head dress.

GOLD CHRISTMAS BOTTLE

DESIGNER: SIMONE McGILLIVRAY

Giving the gift of good cheer in the form of spirits is a grand idea. But don't just hand over a naked bottle. Clothed in gold foil wrapping paper, this handsome soldier deserves to be seen under the tree or on the mantel.

YOU WILL NEED
❖ Gold foil wrapping paper
❖ Gold wire beads
❖ Tape
❖ Scissors

INSTRUCTIONS

1. Roll your bottle up with one edge of the sheet of gold foil paper to measure how wide you will need to cut the paper.

2. Cut the paper to fit the length of the bottle. Gather the extra paper at the bottom of the bottle and tape it flat.

3. Cut two 8-inch (20 cm) squares out of the gold paper.

4. Cut a hole in the middle of the squares. Bring them down over the neck of the bottle one at a time, and gather the edges together to point upwards. Tape them around the neck of the bottle, so that the points remain standing.

5. Wrap approximately 36 inches (92 cm) of gold wire beads around the neck of the bottle.

SHELL AND TISSUE PAPER COLLAGE

DESIGNER: SUSAN KINNEY

*T*his contemporary wrap hints at the ocean and the desert at the same time. Note the shell collage on the front, which is reminiscent of a Georgia O'Keefe painting. The handmade paper adds a touch of the sea.

INSTRUCTIONS

1. Wrap your gift box as usual with a sheet of blue tissue paper. Cut a piece of orange tissue paper narrower than the blue, and long enough to fit around the box lengthwise.

YOU WILL NEED

- ❖ Tissue paper in blue and orange
- ❖ Piece of decorative handmade paper
- ❖ Crab shells and/or other seashells
- ❖ Craft glue
- ❖ Tape
- ❖ Scissors

2. Twist the orange tissue slightly to give it texture, and wrap the strip around the box. Tape the ends in the back.

3. Lay the box down flat and glue a piece of decorative handmade paper in the middle of the twisted orange tissue.

4. Arrange the shells on the decorative paper and glue them down. Allow the collage to dry.

VARIATIONS

Try making your own decorative paper with watercolor. Paint a large piece, which you can cut into smaller pieces after it dries. Store the bits of paper to use as gift cards. You can write on the back.

STAMPED WOODEN BOX

DESIGNER: TRACI NEIL-TAYLOR

A small wooden box, stamped with herbal designs, becomes a keepsake with a simple bit of decoration. Add the stamped seed packets as an extra gift or part of the gift tag.

YOU WILL NEED

- ❖ Wooden box
- ❖ Stamps, in shapes of herbs
- ❖ Green ink pad
- ❖ Coin envelopes (available in office-supply stores)
- ❖ Herb seeds
- ❖ Heavy card stock
- ❖ Twine
- ❖ Pencil
- ❖ Craft glue
- ❖ Deckle-edged scissors

INSTRUCTIONS

1. Measure and mark lightly with a pencil every 2 inches (5 cm) around a wooden box that will fit your gift.

2. Dabbing your herb stamps onto the ink pad, center each stamp over the marks on the box, and press.

3. Stamp the fronts of the coin envelopes with the same stamps.

4. Allow the ink to dry, and fill the envelopes with herb seeds.

5. Cut your card stock with deckle-edged scissors to fit the top of the box. Stamp the center of the card, and allow the ink to dry.

6. Glue the card onto the top of the box.

7. Place a few herb envelopes into the box with your gift. Wrap the twine around the box, and tie at the top.

8. Tuck a few envelopes under the twine on top of the box.

CONSTRUCTIVIST TRIANGLE WRAPPING

DESIGNER: VADIM BORA

*E*ver tried to wrap a triangular object? Well grab those board games, bon-bon boxes, toy packages, and anything else that has been packaged in this hard-to-wrap shape, and follow along. Constructivist design elements borrowed from modern art echo the triangular form of the box, and a funky tie throws a bit of humor into the mix.

YOU WILL NEED

- ❖ Thick commercial paper, (found in office-supply stores)
- ❖ One sheet of decorative paper, black
- ❖ One sheet of decorative paper, red
- ❖ Iridescent hologram wrapping paper
- ❖ Text-weight paper, (for the card)
- ❖ Discarded tie, black or dark color
- ❖ Raffia, black
- ❖ Craft glue
- ❖ Glue brush
- ❖ Ruler
- ❖ Tape
- ❖ Scissors
- ❖ Hole punch

Tip: A scarf or ribbon can be used instead of a tie. The soft material contrasts nicely with the linear, masculine forms of the wrapping.

INSTRUCTIONS

1. Place your triangular package onto the thick neutral colored commercial paper. Cut the paper from the outside edge to the point of the triangle.

2. Fold the paper inward and tape it down, leaving the largest piece to bring over the other folded and taped pieces. Cut the remaining folded over paper to fit the triangle exactly and tape it down.

3. Cut a smaller right angle, approximating the larger triangle, out of the red decorative paper. Brush glue onto the back of the red paper and paste it onto the triangle gift box at a slight angle. Smooth over the paper to ensure that no air bubbles get trapped underneath.

4. Cut a smaller right angle out of the silver hologram paper and glue this on top of the red triangle at a slight angle.

5. Tie the black tie in a traditional knot and slip the loop over the top edge of the triangle. Tighten the knot so that the tie stops one-third of the way down the triangle. Fold the thick part of the tie underneath the bottom edge of the box and affix it in back with tape.

6. For the card, create a smaller version of the giftwrap, stacking the triangles, adding a black triangle for extra dimension. Cut text paper to fit inside the card and glue it inside. Fold the card shut and punch a hole through the top. Thread raffia through the hole and tie it in a bow. Hang the card over the top tip of the triangle.

GOLD AND GLITTER

DESIGNER: BRINDA CALDWELL

Christmas time, especially, is an occasion to pull out all the stops in gift wrapping. Go for the gold, the glitter, the splendor, which may otherwise seem excessive. This gift box will be displayed under a tree or by the fireplace long before it's opened. Then, the brilliant arrangement on top will be removed and used as a table centerpiece.

YOU WILL NEED

- ❖ One sheet of commercial paper, gold
- ❖ Wired ribbon, 4½ inches (11.3 cm) wide, gold and Chinese red
- ❖ Copper wired ribbon, 2 inches (5 cm) wide
- ❖ Wired ribbon, 2½ inches (6.3 cm) wide, gold striped
- ❖ Wired ribbon, 2½ inches (6.3 cm) wide, gold sheer
- ❖ Gold-glitter feathers (available at craft-supply stores)
- ❖ Assorted gold Christmas balls
- ❖ Small gold angel statuette or tree ornament
- ❖ Tape
- ❖ Glue gun and glue sticks
- ❖ Scissors

INSTRUCTIONS

1. Wrap your box as usual with gold paper. Wrap the widest wired ribbon around the box vertically, and glue it to the top.

2. Center the narrower copper ribbon over the wide ribbon, and wrap it over the box. Cut the ends, and glue them to the top.

3. Make several large loops with the wide ribbon, and tie the bundle of loops off at the base. Repeat with the copper and gold sheer ribbon. Make the copper ribbon loops smaller so that they will nestle within the gold striped ribbon and the wide ribbon. Place this in the center of the gold sheer ribbon.

4. Tie a piece of ribbon around the bottom of the bows, and glue the bundle of bows to the top of the box.

5. Tuck the gold-glitter feathers underneath the big bow now topping the box, and glue them down.

6. Evenly disperse the gold balls throughout the bow, and glue them to the ribbon.

7. Place the angel in the center of the bow, and glue it in place.

RED AND BLUE CREPE PAPER CREATION

DESIGNER: BRINDA CALDWELL

The ultimate in party wrapping, crepe paper, with its bold colors and rich texture, always makes a present look festive.

INSTRUCTIONS

1. Wrap your box as usual with the red crepe paper.

2. Cut a wide strip of blue crepe paper, and tie it around the box on each side. Tie the paper strip on the top of the box.

3. Wind the gold and red wire garlands around the box in both directions over the blue crepe paper strip.

4. With the gold and red wire garlands make several large loops and tie them together in the center with the leftover garland wire. Tie the loops to the crepe paper.

5. Curl the ends of the garland wires, and position them as you would like.

6. Cut some stars from scraps of the garlands, and glue them to the paper at random.

YOU WILL NEED

- ❖ 1 sheet of crepe paper, red
- ❖ 1 sheet of crepe paper, blue
- ❖ Gold star wire garland
- ❖ Red star wire garland
- ❖ Tape
- ❖ Craft glue or rubber cement
- ❖ Scissors

GOLD SPONGED WRAPPING

DESIGNER: BRINDA CALDWELL

This impressive hand-decorated paper is easy and fun to create. Add a splashy bow, or present the wrapping unadorned—the hand-sponged design is key here.

INSTRUCTIONS

1. Spread out newsprint in a well-ventilated area, and lightly spray paint your flat sheet of plain paper with the green paint. Allow this to dry.

2. Lightly spray the 18 ct. gold paint over the green, and then the 24 ct. gold paint over the top of that. Allow the paint to dry.

3. Pour the acrylic glaze into a plastic tray, wide enough to dip the sponge. Dip one edge of the sponge into the burgundy glaze, and randomly blot it onto the spray-painted paper. Allow it to dry completely.

4. Wrap your gift with the paper. Wrap your wired ribbon around the box, and tape or glue the ends to the back.

5. Make four large loops in the ribbon, and tie the ends of the bow to the ribbon around the box.

YOU WILL NEED

❖ 1 sheet of plain paper
❖ Can of spray paint, green (basil)
❖ Can of spray paint, 18 ct. gold
❖ Can of spray paint, 24 ct. gold
❖ 1 bottle of acrylic glaze, burgundy
❖ Wired ribbon
❖ Newsprint
❖ Natural sea sponge
❖ Plastic tray for paint
❖ Glue gun and glue sticks
❖ Tape
❖ Scissors

Tips: You can speed the drying process with a blow dryer.

As long as you've got your paints out, make several sheets at once and store them for use later. People will recognize your own signature paper.

FABRIC BOXES

DESIGNER: SANDRA WEBSTER

*M*aking these fabric boxes may take a little practice but the results are well worth it. Enclose a small gift for that someone special, and imagine her delight at the wrapping itself. Make the boxes out of matching napkins, and they are gifts in themselves.

Fabric Boxes

YOU WILL NEED

❖ 2 pieces of sturdy fabric, approximately 18 inches (46 cm) square (the size may vary)

INSTRUCTIONS

1. Lay the fabric flat, with the printed side down, and press the top third down and the bottom third up over it.

2. Flip the piece over by bringing the top edge toward you.

3. Estimate the halfway point of the piece of fabric, and fold the right edge to the "halfway mark." This is only a temporary fold, so don't crease it.

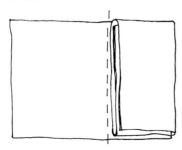

4. Bring the left side over to the folded edge on the right.

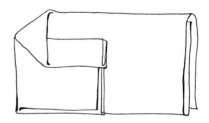

5. Unfold the right-hand fold back out, and bring the top one-third of the left-hand fold section down by one-third. There will be a triangular fold to the left. Press this down.

6. Bring the bottom third of the same section up and over this fold and press down. It will also have a triangular fold below the first one.

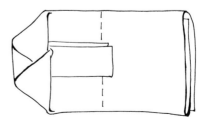

7. Gently fold the tail created by the new folds over the triangular folds to the left.

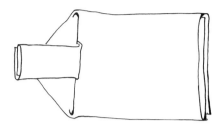

8. Bring the right edge of the folded fabric over to match up with the extended ends. Repeat steps 5 and 6 with this side of fabric. Turn the new folded tail out to the right. Your fabric should look like the illustration below.

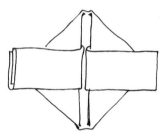

9. Place your thumbs under the two tails where they fold away from the center, and gently turn the box inside out so that the tails overlap on the inside of the box. Do not let the folds come undone as you turn the fabric inside out. Make sure that the walls of the box are even and the corners as crisp as possible.

10. Repeat these steps with another piece of fabric. Fit one over the other like a lid, and your box is done.

Double-Pocket Package

YOU WILL NEED
❖ Two pieces of fabric, 12 inches square
❖ String

INSTRUCTIONS

1. Place the fabric with the printed side down, and fold up one third of the fabric from the bottom. Press it down.

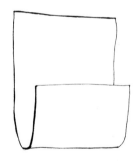

2. Turn the fabric over, keeping the pressed fold intact.

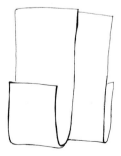

3. Fold the fabric into thirds, left side first, then the right side over the rest. Bring down the top edges even with the bottom of the fabric.

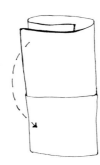

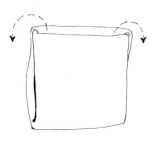

4. You should now have a square with a pocket on the back. Placing your fingers inside the pocket and your thumbs outside, gently turn the pocket inside out.

5. Push out the corners to neaten the pocket. It should look like the illustration at right.

6. Make another pocket to fit into the side pocket of the first one that you made, following steps 1 through 5. The second pocket will keep the raw edges to the back side of the package.

7. Tie a matching string around the pocket.

Sentimental Emergency Wrap

DESIGNER: ANNIE CICALE

Trying to think of something inventive and unusual as decoration for a gift to grandma or your favorite aunt? Something sweetly sentimental for your husband or wife?

These colorful wrappings are so easy, and they convey just the right personal touch. Preserve your children's first ABC's, first letters from camp, or first drawings. Give a meaningful letter to a loved-one, a hand-written poem to a lover—all gently enveloping a chosen gift within.

To recreate these colorful bundles of joy, simply photocopy your works of art on color paper. Use the different sizes available in your copier.

Grab a few photographs from your desk, postcards from a colleague, or create a collage with office supplies, using paper clips, rulers, pencils, floppy disks. Place the objects on the copier plate and cover them with a blank sheet of paper, press the copy button, and voilà—a whimsically creative wrapping.

Match colorful bows to your wrapping.

CRANE-OF-HAPPINESS WRAP

DESIGNER: PEI-LING BECKER

*A*sian gift-wrapping traditions indicate that a small portion of the gift should be visible. Add an origami crane, which represents happiness, as a decoration and the gift wrapping is complete.

YOU WILL NEED

❖ 1 sheet of thick, textured hand-made paper

❖ 1 sheet of contrasting paper

❖ Origami paper or flexible handmade paper

❖ Dried flowers

❖ Raffia

❖ Tape

INSTRUCTIONS

1. If your gift is a bundle of objects, such as incense, pencils, or tapers, tie them together in the middle first. Add a dried flower at each end.

2. Wrap the bundle with a piece of thick textured paper, cut to allow each end of the bundle to show. Tape the paper on the back of the bundle, where one side overlaps the other.

3. Wrap another layer of contrasting paper over the first textured paper, and tape it.

4. Wrap raffia around the middle of the wrapped bundle, and tie it into a knot.

5. Make an origami crane (see the instructions on page 121), and attach it to the raffia knot.

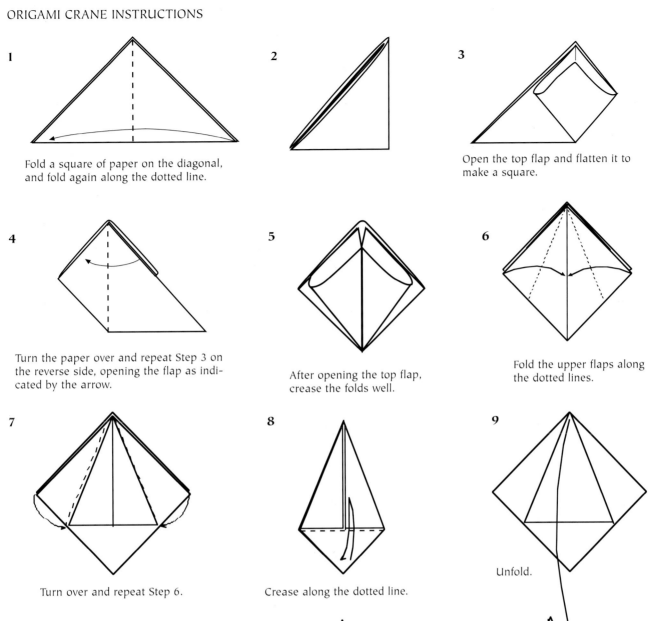

1

Fold a square of paper on the diagonal, and fold again along the dotted line.

2

3

Open the top flap and flatten it to make a square.

4

Turn the paper over and repeat Step 3 on the reverse side, opening the flap as indicated by the arrow.

5

After opening the top flap, crease the folds well.

6

Fold the upper flaps along the dotted lines.

7

Turn over and repeat Step 6.

8

Crease along the dotted line.

9

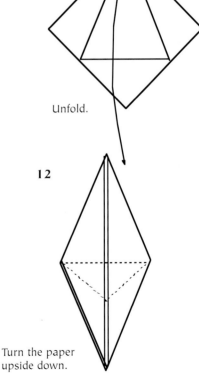

Unfold.

10

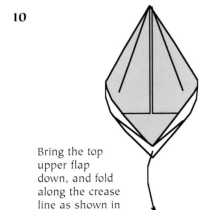

Bring the top upper flap down, and fold along the crease line as shown in Step 11.

11

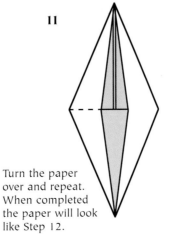

Turn the paper over and repeat. When completed the paper will look like Step 12.

12

Turn the paper upside down.

13

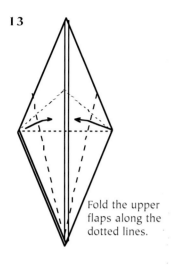

Fold the upper flaps along the dotted lines.

14

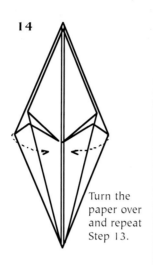

Turn the paper over and repeat Step 13.

15

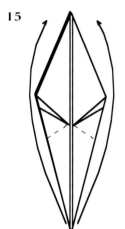

Open and flatten the bottom flaps by bringing them up and folding along the dotted lines while reversing the previous folds.

16

To make the beak, open one tip, then push it in to flatten and reverse the fold.

17

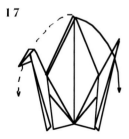

Open the wings by folding them down.

18

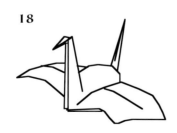

GILDED PAPER WRAP

DESIGNER: SUSAN KINNEY

*T*he handmade paper in this project displays both texture and richness in color. Combined with geometric folds and a ribbon made of tissue paper, the results are both sleek and harmonious.

INSTRUCTIONS

1. Cut the sheet of gilded paper, leaving an extra 2 inches (5 cm) in width to be folded over later. Wrap your present, but don't tape it yet. Flip the package over and use what is usually the underside as the top.

2. Measure a piece of gold tissue paper 4 inches (10 cm) wide and the length of the other paper to fit your package. Fold the paper in half lengthwise, so that you have a long, narrow strip of tissue.

3. Tuck the tissue paper between the gilded paper where it meets lengthwise on the box, folded side out.

YOU WILL NEED

- ❖ 1 sheet of dark paper with gilded metallic highlights (available in art-supply stores)
- ❖ 1 sheet of gold tissue paper
- ❖ Thin-gauge wire
- ❖ Set of chopsticks
- ❖ Variously shaped beads
- ❖ Tape
- ❖ Scissors

4. Leave ½ inch (1.3 cm) of the tissue paper showing, and tape it over the bottom half of the gilded paper, which is already folded over the gift.

5. Bring the other half of the gilded paper over the tissue paper and fold the edge back onto itself, so that approximately 1 inch (2.5 cm) of the underside shows, and tape down. (**Tip:** For the best results, use double-sided tape affixed to the underside of the gilded paper.)

6. Measure around your box horizontally, and cut a 2-inch wide (5 cm) strip of gold tissue paper, long enough to fit around the box.

7. Fold the tissue in half lengthwise or twist it to achieve a decorative look. Wrap the tissue around the top third of the box, and tape the ends together underneath the package.

8. Wrap the thin-gauge wire around the package, following the line of the gold tissue paper, ending on top of the package.

9. Twist a loop around a set of chopsticks with the wire, where the tissue and wire "ribbon" meet. Cut the wire.

10. Cut two 4-inch-long (10 cm) pieces of wire. At one end of each wire, twist a loop, which will keep the beads from falling off.

11. String two small beads of differing colors and one larger bead onto each wire. Wrap the ends of the wire around the intersection of the wire "ribbon" and the chopsticks.

GIFT TAGS

DESIGNER: STEPHANIE ELLIS

*H*ere are three unique gift tags, using hand-painted and handmade paper.

Envelope Card

INSTRUCTIONS

1. Fold the text-weight paper in half, and set aside.

2. Fold a piece of decorative paper, measuring 3¾ x 10 inches (9.5 x 26 cm), 3½ inches (9 cm) from the left, and again at 3¾ inches (9.5 cm), and open flat.

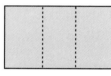

3. On the right vertical edge, mark ¾ inch (2 cm) down from the top and up from the bottom. Make a diagonal cut from the mark to the edge of the first crease with your craft knife.

4. Fold the decorative paper to form an envelope. Make two small pencil marks 1 inch (2.5 cm) from the top of the folded envelope on both sides of the fold-over flap. Unfold the envelope, and using your ruler as a straightedge, cut between the two pencil marks with the craft knife.

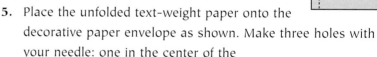

5. Place the unfolded text-weight paper onto the decorative paper envelope as shown. Make three holes with your needle: one in the center of the crease and one at ¼ inch (6 mm) from each edge of the text-weight paper.

6. Thread your needle with waxed linen thread, and insert the needle into the

center hole from the outside of the card, leaving a tail. Bring the needle back through the bottom hole. Re-enter the center hole, and bring the needle back through the top hole. Tie a small knot at the center opening with the remaining thread and leftover tail.

Tri-Fold Card

INSTRUCTIONS

1. Fold your text-weight paper 2 inches (5 cm) from each end.

2. Fold a piece of decorative paper, measuring 3¾ x 7¼ inches (9.5 x 18.5 cm), 2 inches (5 cm) from each end.

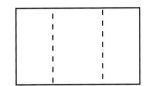

3. Sew the two sheets of paper together following the directions in the previous design.

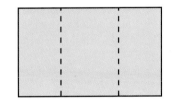

Folded Envelope Card

INSTRUCTIONS

1. Fold your text-weight paper in half.

2. Place the folded text-weight paper, measuring 6 inches square (15 cm square), inside the decorated paper diagonally. Fold the corners of the decorative paper inward.

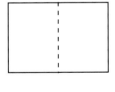

3. Sew or glue the text-weight paper to the decorative paper.

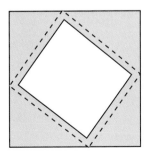

Templates

Vellum Envelope (a) (p.105)

Vellum Envelope (b) (p.105)

Vellum Envelope (c) (p.105)

Corrugated Cardboard Gift Box (p. 90)

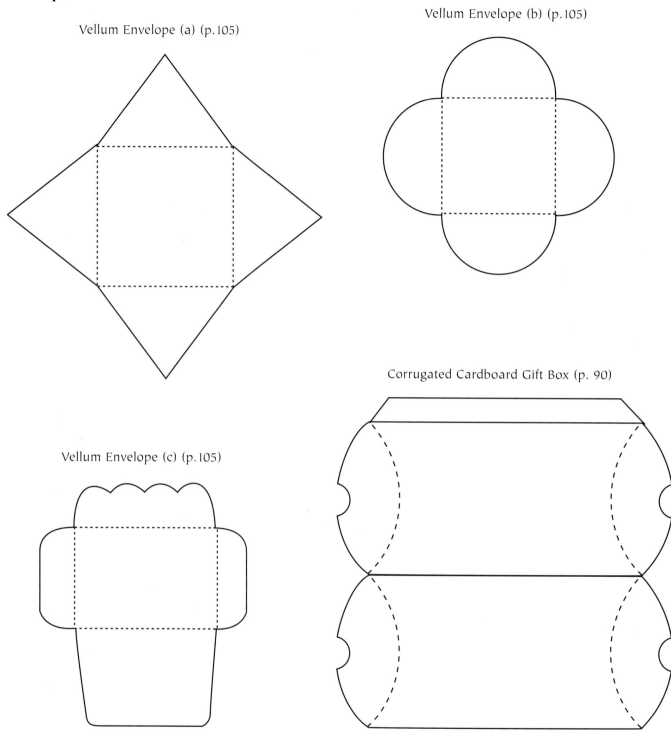

CONTRIBUTING DESIGNERS

Pei-Ling Becker creates original paper art, ranging from jewelry to wall-hangings to three-dimensional paper sculpture. Since coming to the United States in 1988 from Taiwan, she has won numerous awards and has participated in many exhibitions. She resides in Black Mountain, NC.

Vadim Bora is a fine artist, sculptor, and painter. His background includes interior, architectural, and jewelry design. In the applied arts, he masterfully modernizes the ancient artistic traditions of various cultures. Originally from the northern Caucasus Mountains in Ossetia, he has brought the rich heritage of his culture to the mountains of North Carolina. He owns Vadim Bora Studio-Gallery in downtown Asheville, where he continues his artistic endeavors and cultural exchange.

Barbara Bussolari is a retired Massachusetts high school teacher, now living in the mountains of North Carolina. For the past 20 years, she has designed, made, and sold cards using handmade and hand-decorated papers and hand-woven material. She is now exploring and expanding into paper jewelry and dolls made with hand-woven material and handmade papers.

Brinda Caldwell is a floral artist with a flair for the elegant and unusual. She has taught floral design for seven years and enjoys learning as much as the students do. She specializes in weddings and decorating large facilities, and is the owner of The Tiger Lily in Asheville, NC.

Annie Cicale holds degrees in chemical engineering and art, including an MFA in graphic design. She has worked as an engineer and an art teacher, but in 1981 she turned to full-time studio work, supplemented by a good deal of teaching. She has taught at universities in Montana, at Paier College of Art in Hamden, CT, and at 12 international calligraphy conferences, as well as for societies throughout the U.S. and Canada. She is a juried member of the Southern Highland Craft Guild and is publications director for the International Association of Calligraphic Arts.

Stephanie Ellis is originally from Charlotte, NC, where she received a Bachelor of Fine Arts Degree from the University of North Carolina at Charlotte. She now resides in Asheville, NC, where she paints, makes handmade paper, journals, and cards. She also works in a screen-printing studio, allowing her to combine her interests in painting and paper arts with the screen-printing process.

Constance Ensner has operated "Constance Boutique", in downtown Asheville, NC, since 1984. Her creative impulses are sporadically expressed in sewing (with a good deal of training in tailoring, pattern drafting, and design) and in displays within the store.

Myrna Harrigan has been an interior decorator in Chicago for over 15 years and recently relocated to Arden, NC, where she continues her decorating business.

Dana Heldreth lives in Asheville, NC, with her husband, three children, four cats, an iguana, and a snake. She spends most of her time chasing after her one-year-old daughter.

Corinne (Corky) Kurzmann is living an eclectic life in Asheville, NC, with her five sons and three hounds. She loves gardening, teaching, living, and chaos, not necessarily in that order...or in any order.

Traci Neil-Taylor loves diversity. As well as being an artist, she is also a caterer and a massage therapist. She works and lives in Asheville, NC, with her husband Treavis.

Maggie Rotman is an artist who works in fiber. She lives in Asheville, NC.

Simone McGillivray is a vocalist and classical musician, currently pursuing further studies in Greensboro, NC. She has a natural flair for interior design and artistry in many fields.

Lisa Sanders has designed lingerie for 15 years for major brand names. She has traveled the world over and is currently a free-lance designer working in apparel, home furnishings, and crafts.

Molly Sieburg has a background in painting and floral design. She currently uses her abilities at the Gardener's Cottage, a flower/garden/antique store, in Asheville, NC, where she is part-owner and responsible for most of the buying and all of the displays.

Carol Stangler is an environmental artist who creates baskets and sculptures from vines, bark, grasses, and other natural materials. She lives and works in Asheville, NC.

Patrice Tappé is an opera singer and co-owner of Art International Asheville, a fine arts gallery, with her husband, Clayton Wefel, in Asheville, NC.

Sandy Webster is an artist currently working in mixed media. She received her BFA from Western Carolina University and is presently working on her MFA. Her works have appeared throughout the U.S. in publications, juried and invitational exhibitions. Sandy has taught, lectured and juried on fiber related workshops and exhibits throughout the U.S., Canada, and Australia. Her students are encouraged to try the possibilities while exploring technique, color, design, and content.

Index